An Early Start to Nature

Roy Richards

SIMON & SCHUSTER

LONDON • SYDNEY • NEW YORK • TOKYO • TORONTO

Text © Roy Richards 1989
Design and artwork © Simon and Schuster 1989

First published in Great Britain in 1989 by
Simon & Schuster Ltd
Wolsey House, Wolsey Road
Hemel Hempstead HP2 4SS

Reprinted 1990

Printed in Great Britain by
BPCC Paulton Books Ltd

British Library Cataloguing in Publication Data

Richards, Roy
  An early start to nature
  1. Primary schools curriculum subjects:
  Science – For teaching.
  I.Title
  372.3'5
  ISBN 0-7501-0044-3

Series editor: John Day
Editor: Elizabeth Clarke
Design: Jerry Watkiss and David Bryant/Joan
        Farmer Artists
Artwork: Nicola Armstrong pages 17, 19(T), 29,
          30, 33-35, 48, 56
          Anna Hancock pages 12, 15, 16, 19(B),
          23, 36-38, 40, 42, 44, 46, 49-51,
          53-55
          David Bryant/Joan Farmer Artists (all
          other artwork)
Photographs: Alan Barker (pages 8 and 13)
             Frank Lane Picture Agency
             (page 22)

This book is a companion volume to An Early Start to Science. I had originally intended that it be largely for teachers of children in first schools, but in its execution it quickly became clear that it is a book which can be used across the whole primary age range. It is suitable wherever children are beginning to explore the natural world.

The emphasis is on practical investigation at first hand and the book suggests many things to do. While factual information is occasionally given, it is not intended that the book be used as an identification guide. There are many good identification books on the market and the activities suggested in this book will often turn children to using them. Like An Early Start to Science, the activities are intended to promote:

☐ **exploration** *of the environment in order to gain experience at first hand*

☐ **manipulation** *of objects and materials*

☐ **observation** *of things around children*

☐ **comparison** *of things, one with another*

☐ **questioning** *and arguing about things*

☐ **testing** *things out and indulging in simple problem-solving activities*

☐ **looking at pattern** *and seeking relationships in the data collected*

The illustrations show the kinds of things and materials needed for the investigations. I have deliberately eschewed the use of sophisticated apparatus and have concentrated on using the everyday things around children, since these are unlikely to come between children and understanding.

In addition, manipulative and thinking skills are employed in devising and constructing a piece of apparatus, or setting up a sound experimental situation.

Over and above all this, lies the caring attitude which can be caught from the teacher where a proper respect for living things is shown. Time and again in this work it is necessary to point out to children that plants should only be collected where there are many and then only a few should be taken; that both plants and animals be housed and looked after carefully; and that animals be returned quickly to their natural environment. Children can show a genuine care, concern and sensitivity for living things, and a feeling for conservation – but this needs to be nurtured.

From experience I would suggest that exploration of the natural world has become neglected in some schools over recent years. The concepts that children can grasp from such study are profound and important. They are concepts embedded in a world of immense interest to children. Young children are closer to the earth than adults, both physically and by their nature, and they take a natural delight in a wriggling worm, a butterfly emerging from its cocoon, the discovery of a bird's nest, or a fish darting in a stream. Their delight has always been my delight and I hope it will be yours, too, as you explore the natural world with them. Bon voyage.

Basic ideas in natural science

There are many basic concepts that children will encounter as they explore the natural world. Many of these will take time for children to understand but the experiences leading towards such understanding are present in the activities suggested in this book. Of these concepts some of the most important ones touched on are:

Interdependence   Living things depend on each other in various ways.

Food chains   Some animals eat plants and some eat other animals but all animals ultimately depend on green plants.

Adaptation   Living things are usually well suited in form and function to their natural environment.

Variation   No two living things are identical in all respects. Even within one species there are differences.

Life needs   Most living things need water, air and nourishment for life processes.

Reproduction   Living things produce offspring of the same kind.

Senses   Animals have senses of sight, sound, hearing, taste and smell which provide different information about the environment.

Classification   Animals, plants and materials can be sorted on the basis of different criteria into groups, sets or collections.

Environment   In any situation there are many variable conditions all in operation at the same time. These can affect and modify places and their inhabitants.

Seasons   Changes in the physical environment due to seasonal cycles are often matched by changes or events in the living world.

Soil   This is a mixture of things coming from rocks and living things. Substances taken from the soil by plants during growth must be replaced to maintain fertility.

Solar system   The apparent movements of the sun, moon and stars follow a regular pattern.

Print making gives interesting, effective records. It also focuses attention on form, develops appreciation of plant structure, develops manipulative skills, and encourages careful observation.

Things needed

Scribble painting

This is easier with simple leaves rather than divided ones.

Recently shed autumn leaves can soon be dried and hardened, and are ideal for making prints.

Put the leaf on a newspaper, lower surface up.

Cover with a white sheet (medium thickness).

Hold the paper firmly so that the leaf does not slip. Rub with a crayon, making sure that you do edges, stalks and veins well. You could try scribbles in pencil, too.

Cut out the leaf print and mount on coloured paper or card.

Bark rubbing

Choose youngish bark, free from moss or lichen, that shows a characteristic pattern. Typing, tracing and greaseproof paper are suitable for rubbings. Tinted paper gives more striking results.

Choose your tree carefully.

Oak has widely-spaced ridges which stand out in a rubbing, leaving blank spaces where the fissures occur. Lime has diamond-shaped lenticels, running in rows up and down the trunk. Holly gives little dots and dashes all over the rubbing.

You can also use a candle and colour in the unwaxed parts of the paper. This shows up the fissures in the bark.

Boot polish prints

Brown, tan and reddish boot polishes can often match the colour in autumn leaves.

Smear the lower surface of the leaf with polish, using a wad of cotton wool or a finger. Spread evenly and sparingly.

Place the leaf (polish-side down) on a sheet of white paper. Cover it with another sheet of paper.

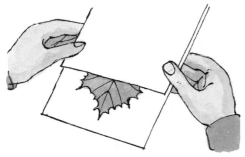

Rub gently on the top bit of paper. Lift the leaf to leave a coloured print.

You can use poster paints instead of boot polish. Here you can match reds, greens and yellows to the appropriate parts of the leaf.

Carbon paper prints

Rub firmly and evenly all over the leaf. Then cut out the leaf print and mount it.

Alternatively, the underside of the leaf can be coated with carbon paper and a print made as with boot polish prints.

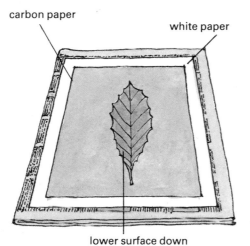

carbon paper

white paper

lower surface down

Soot prints

Lightly smear a saucer with Vaseline. Hold the coated surface over a candle flame.

Move the saucer around until the surface is coated with soot.

Press the lower surface of the leaf on to the soot.

Then press on to white paper.

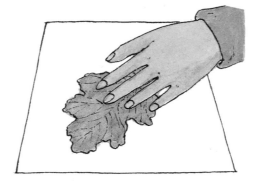

Spatter prints

This technique gives very attractive leaf outlines. These can be used, for example, as cover designs for stitched books or as wall-mounted pictures.

Place a leaf on to a sheet of white paper, using plenty of newspaper for protection.

Run the blade of a blunt knife over the bristles of a paint-covered toothbrush to flick the paint.

Now remove the leaf to reveal the white silhouette.

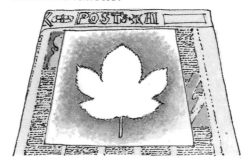

Sorting and separating leaf prints

Which leaves are small?
Which are large?
Which are simple?
Which are made up of leaflets?
Which have lots of veins?
Which have few?
Which are smooth?
Which are wrinkled?
Which have smooth edges?
Which have serrated edges?

This is best done with hard materials such as winter twigs, sycamore or rose fruits, and evergreen leaves, such as ivy.

Imprints

Some regions, such as Greater London, have a clay soil. This can be dug up, washed, and used for making imprints. You can also use Plasticine.

Play with the clay and mould it into a soft ball.

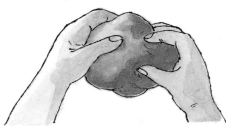

Flatten the clay on a board and cut it into rectangular pieces.

Press a twig firmly into the clay, leaving a short piece sticking out.

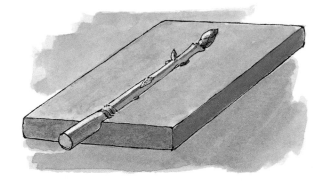

Lift the twig by the protruding end.

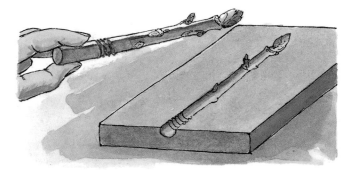

The impression can be used as a mould to make a plaster replica.

Make 'fossil imprints'

You can make 'fossil imprints' with shells or fishbones.

You could compare these with real fossil imprints, if these are available.

Casts

Take a strip of card, 4 cm wide. Fit it around your clay tile bearing the impression. Allow for an overlap on one side.

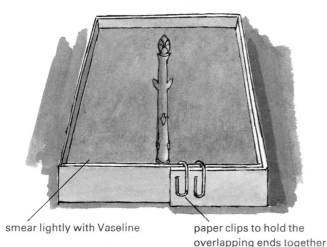

smear lightly with Vaseline

paper clips to hold the overlapping ends together

Mix some plaster of Paris (dental plaster is best) by adding the plaster powder to the water. Stir all the time, until the mixture is the consistency of double cream.

Don't delay once it is ready. Pour it straight into the mould, filling it level with the top. Tap the sides gently to remove air bubbles, which would otherwise weaken the cast.

Leave overnight. Then peel away the card and remove the clay base.

Paint and label your cast. Use natural colours with a contrasting background.

Casts of footprints

Start with a tray of firm, damp sand.

Make a footprint.

Press a strip of card into the sand.

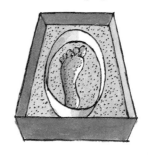

Pour in the plaster of Paris.

Clean your hardened cast with an old toothbrush.

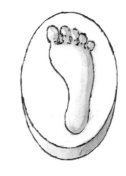

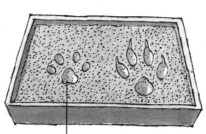

cat (retracted claws)

Try taking prints of cats and dogs to make casts.

There are many ways of measuring the heights of trees. Here are a few suggestions.

Rough estimate

Ask a child to stand by a tree. Estimate how many times the child's height goes into the tree. Multiply this number by the child's height to find the height of the tree.

Taking photographs

To make a more accurate measurement, take a photograph of a child standing by the side of a tree. Knowing the height of the child, it is easy to work out the height of the tree.

Take the following example.

True height of Susan = 120 cm
Height of Susan in photo = 1.5 cm
Height of tree in photo = 6 cm

In the photograph

$$\frac{\text{Height of tree}}{120\ cm} = \frac{6\ cm}{1.5\ cm}$$

So, true height of tree $= \frac{6 \times 120}{1.5}$ cm

$$= 480\ cm = 4.8\ m$$

Using a ruler

Another rough estimation method is to sight on a child by holding up a ruler. Move your thumb along the ruler until distance AB corresponds to the child's height.

Now estimate how many times distance AB goes into the height of the tree. Multiply this by the child's height to get the height of the tree.

Alternative ruler method

Use a ruler to get a sighting AB. Keep your thumb firmly on B and swing the ruler anticlockwise to meet the ground level at C.

Ask a child to place a peg at C. The distance BC should give you the approximate height of the tree.

Bending over

Bend over and look between your legs. Move forward until the top of the tree can be seen through your legs. The distance AB should give you an approximation of the height.

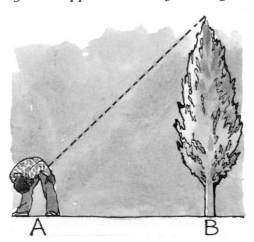

Casting shadows

This is effective where the tree being measured casts a shadow from its top. Therefore a poplar is better for this method than a more spreading tree, such as an oak. Use the shadow of a metre stick to compare with the shadow from the tree.

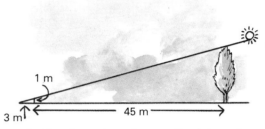

As the drawing shows, the triangles are similar. Thus the ratio of two adjacent sides in one triangle will be the same as that for the corresponding sides in the other triangle.

Therefore

$$\frac{\text{Height of tree}}{45\ m} = \frac{1\ m}{3\ m}$$

Height of tree $= \frac{45}{3}$ m

$$= 15\ m$$

Make a gauge

Use a strip of thick card to make your gauge. Hold your gauge at arm's length and sight on a tree. Move away until the gauge seems just to overlap the top and base of the tree.

Ask a child to stick a piece of tape on the trunk of the tree to coincide with the notch in the gauge.

gauge tape

The height of the tree is roughly ten times the height of the tape above the ground.

Use a plumb bob

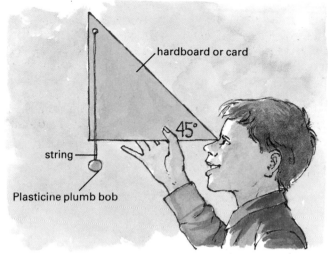

hardboard or card

string

Plasticine plumb bob

45°

Sight along the longest side of the card triangle. Use the vertically hanging plumb bob to ensure you are holding the triangle vertically. Walk away from the tree until you can line up the top of the tree with the longest side of your card triangle.

The height of the tree will then be the distance of the tree from you (A), plus your height (B).

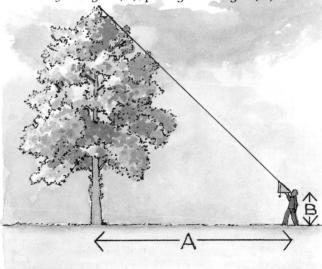

Make a clinometer

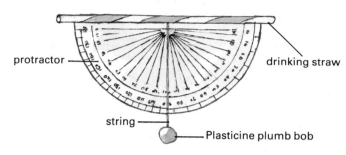

protractor

drinking straw

string

Plasticine plumb bob

Measure a distance of 30 metres from a tree. Sight on the top of your tree through the drinking straw attached to the clinometer.

The height of the tree at this distance is shown in this table.

Angle (degrees)	Height above eye level (metres)
5	2.6
10	5.3
15	8.0
20	11.0
25	14.0
30	17.3
35	21.0
40	25.2
45	30.0

Estimate lengths for angles between those given.

Recording results

Measure tree heights by different methods and keep a record.

Approx. height of trees	method			
	1	2	3	4
oak				
poplar				

What observations do children make about their results?

Tree leaf area

Try estimating the number of leaves on a deciduous tree. The beginning of the summer term is a good time to do this.

Count the number of leaves on a branch and the number of branches on the tree. Multiply the two together to get the total number of leaves.

Take one branch and pick a sample of 30 leaves (ten large, ten medium and ten small).

Work out the total leaf area of these 30 leaves by drawing their outlines on squared paper and counting the squares.

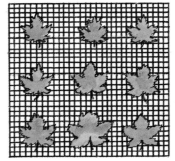

Divide the total number of leaves on the whole tree by 30. Multiply the answer by the area of the 30 leaves to find the total leaf area of the tree.

Take the following example.

Total number of leaves = 9000
Area of sample of 30 leaves = 600 sq cm
Therefore total leaf area =

$$\frac{9000 \times 600}{30} = 180\,000 \text{ sq cm}$$

Repeating this exercise at the end of the summer term will illustrate the enormous increase in photosynthetic tissue that occurs during the summer.

Changing leaf colour

This is a task for the autumn. Hold a sheet of plain paper, attached to a clip-board, behind a low-hanging leaf on a deciduous tree.

Make several traces of the outline of your leaf. Don't pull the leaf from the tree and be careful not to damage it.

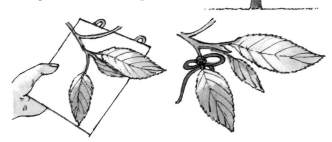

Mark it with a piece of coloured wool, tied gently around the stalk. Now colour one of your leaf outlines to match the colours in the leaf.

Watch the leaf from day to day. Make a pictorial record, dating each drawing.

16th Sept   22nd Sept   29th Sept
15th Oct   24th Oct   28th Oct

You could make a written record.

Tree	Colour of leaves		
	Sept	Oct	Nov
Oak			
Cherry			
Plane			
Rowan			

You could make such records for a number of deciduous trees and contrast the results. Trees of the same species tend to go through the same pattern of colour changes, although each tree changes at its own rate.

Trees of different species go through different colour changes.

Ideas children can meet

The leaf canopy increases during summer to provide more photosynthetic tissue. As a leaf dies, the internal tissues break down, resulting in a change of pigmentation.

Looking at the tree canopy

Walk around under a tree and try to mark the outside edge of the tree canopy with PE skittles. It helps for someone to stand away from the tree and give directions.

The distance from the trunk to a marker can be measured in paces or metres. Angles from the trunk to each marker can be estimated (a board protractor is a useful aid).

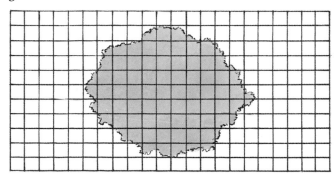

Now plot the shape of the canopy on graph paper. One centimetre square for each metre square is a good scale.

Does the vegetation outside the canopy differ from that within the canopy?

Sun and shade

*Stand under a tree on a sunny day.
How does it feel compared with the open?
Use a thermometer to take temperatures in the shade and in the open. Try to take temperatures at hourly intervals throughout the day.*

*Now try measuring temperatures under different tree species. Does the temperature vary?
Which trees cast the most dense shadow?*

Measure seasonal increase in leaf cover

Monitor a tree during the spring and early summer when leaf growth is most rapid. Choose a deciduous tree. It should be an isolated tree.

Place a large sheet of paper (pinned to a drawing board) on the ground under your tree. Draw around the shadows cast on the paper, to get an idea of the leaf cover.

Look at the spaces between the leaf shadows to estimate the amount of light filtering through the leaves.

*Do this again at monthly intervals to contrast the amounts of leaf cover.
Try to take your readings at the same time each day.*

Date	mid March	mid April	mid May
sun and shade patterns			
number of leaves	no leaves	leaves opened by 2 weeks	full leaf cover
estimation of spaces between leaves			

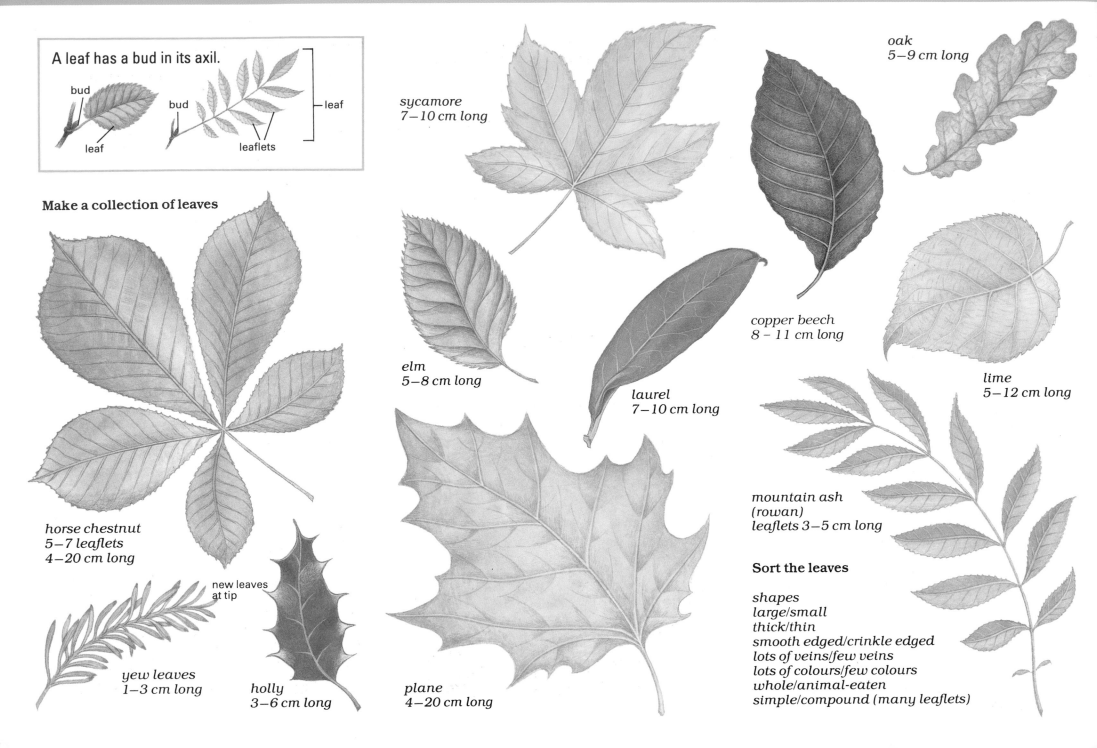

A leaf has a bud in its axil.

bud

leaf

bud

leaflets

leaf

Make a collection of leaves

sycamore
7−10 cm long

oak
5−9 cm long

copper beech
8 − 11 cm long

elm
5−8 cm long

laurel
7−10 cm long

lime
5−12 cm long

horse chestnut
5−7 leaflets
4−20 cm long

new leaves
at tip

mountain ash
(rowan)
leaflets 3−5 cm long

yew leaves
1−3 cm long

holly
3−6 cm long

plane
4−20 cm long

Sort the leaves

shapes
large/small
thick/thin
smooth edged/crinkle edged
lots of veins/few veins
lots of colours/few colours
whole/animal-eaten
simple/compound (many leaflets)

Pressing leaves

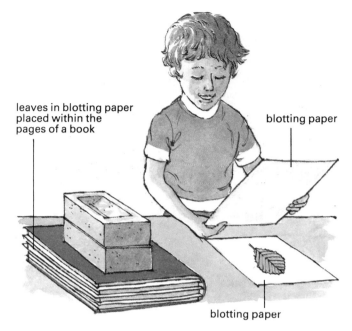

leaves in blotting paper placed within the pages of a book

blotting paper

blotting paper

Alternatively, you could press your leaves between layers of newspaper beneath the carpet.

Mount your pressed leaves in a book to make an identification guide to local trees.

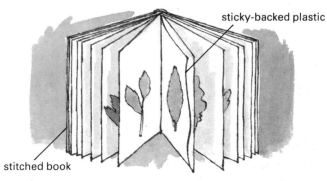

sticky-backed plastic

stitched book

Or you could make a wall display of your pressed leaves, sticking them to cardboard with sticky-backed plastic.

You can temporarily preserve dry leaves by ironing them between sheets of waxed paper.

Hang the sheets in a window so that the light can filter through them.

Looking at leaf skeletons

Some trees, such as magnolias, produce very good leaf skeletons. Search in autumn beneath the shrubs and make a collection. Try to identify the skeletons.

Here is a good specimen.

Make your own leaf skeletons

This should be done only by teachers since caustic substances are used.

Add 50 g of washing soda to one pint of water and add 25 g of quicklime. Bring the mixture to the boil. Remove from the heat and cool. Carefully pour off the clear liquid from the sediment.

Soak the leaves in the decanted liquid for an hour. Watch them carefully – some leaves need less time and will disintegrate if left too long. Remove the leaves and place them on a sheet of newspaper to dry.

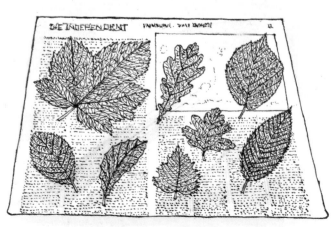

Measure a tree's girth

Join hands around the trunk. Some big trees may need two or three children to measure them in this way.

Using pieces of string, you can get fairly accurate measurements of the girth.

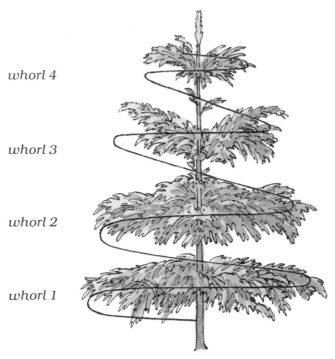

Measure the girth at different heights above ground-level to see how much the trunk tapers. Do this with different species and make a chart to show your results.

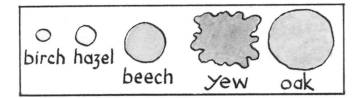

birch hazel beech yew oak

Measure a tree's diameter

You can make a simple caliper from a metre rule.

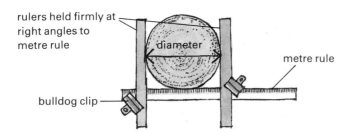

rulers held firmly at right angles to metre rule

diameter

metre rule

bulldog clip

How old is this tree?

You can work out the age of a conifer by counting the whorls as you go up the tree.

whorl 4

whorl 3

whorl 2

whorl 1

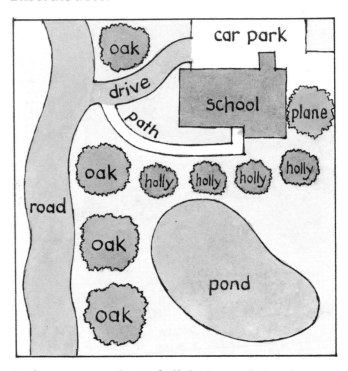

The typical deciduous tree in the open increases its girth by about 2.5 cm each year. This is only a rough estimate.

Measure the girth of your deciduous tree about 1.5 m from the ground. Divide this by 2.5 cm to give you the age of the tree.

For example, if the girth is 250 cm, the tree's age will be

$$\frac{250}{2.5} = 100 \ years$$

Woodland trees are more shaded. So their girth increases by only about 1.5 cm each year.

Do a tree census

Survey the trees in your school grounds or local park. Make a sketch map of the school, putting in the roads and paths and other main features. Label the trees.

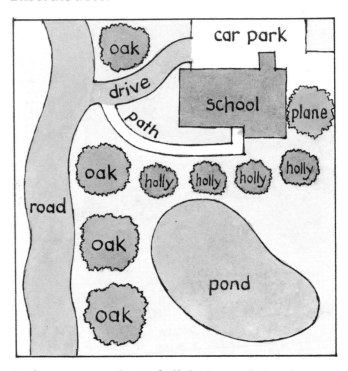

Make a census chart of all the trees. A simple one like this will do.

TREE	1	2	3	4
oak				
holly				
plane				

Animal life in trees

Do this towards the end of the summer term. Oak and birch are best, while plane trees give poor results.

Hit a low-lying branch with a stout stick. Any small animals will fall on to the white sheet, together with lots of leaf debris. Carefully pick up the catch with plastic spoons and paint brushes.

Examine your finds. Identify and talk about the animals.

Caterpillars, especially 'looper' caterpillars, and spiders are the most common types. Caterpillars will be feeding on the leaves. Spiders are carnivorous.

After your inspection return all the animals to the tree.

Looking at winged fruit

Collect winged fruit from sycamore, maple and ash.

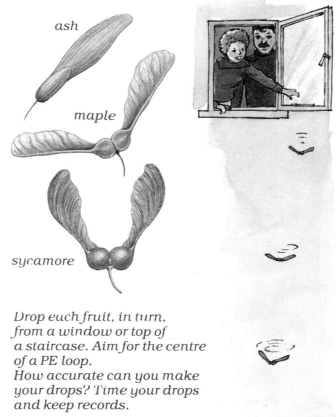

ash

maple

sycamore

Drop each fruit, in turn, from a window or top of a staircase. Aim for the centre of a PE loop.
How accurate can you make your drops? Time your drops and keep records.

See if the results are any different when damaged fruits are used.

Fruit	time of drop	average
Sycamore	1	
	2	
	3	
Ash	1	
	2	
	3	

Make your own 'winged fruits'

You can simulate winged fruit by making paper cut-outs.

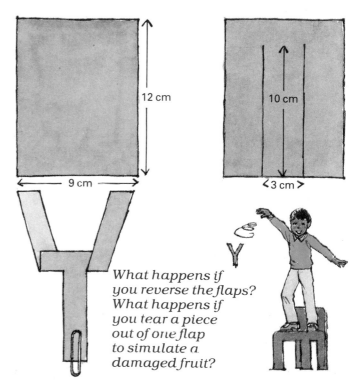

What happens if you reverse the flaps? What happens if you tear a piece out of one flap to simulate a damaged fruit?

How far do fruits and seeds fall?

Find the parent tree and see how widely spread the fruits are. The horse chestnut fruit splits to release a shiny brown seed, the conker, which can roll some way. Winged fruits can be carried hundreds of metres.

Children can easily sort flowers into groups based solely on looking at the petals. Such groupings can be the basis of an interesting and attractive flower book.

Petals from small flowers can be stuck under sticky-backed plastic. Flower catalogue pictures are useful for the larger flowers.

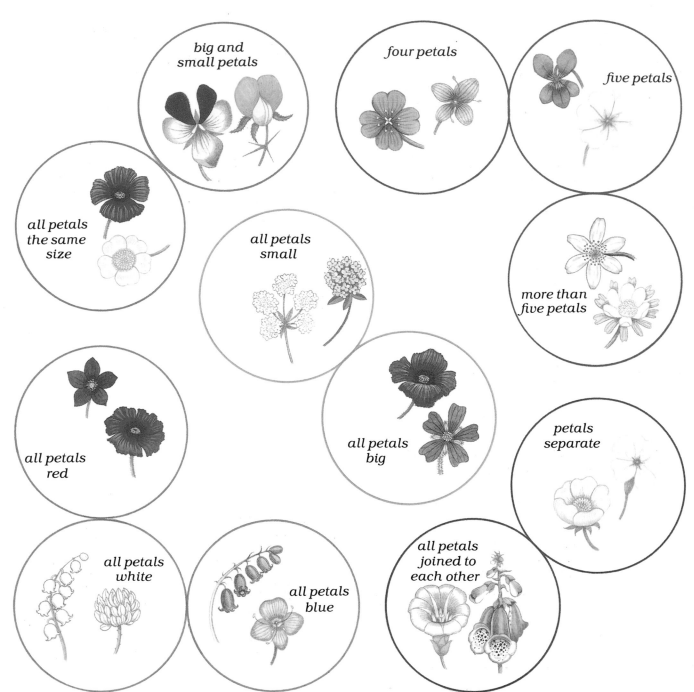

big and small petals

four petals

five petals

all petals the same size

all petals small

more than five petals

all petals red

all petals big

petals separate

all petals white

all petals blue

all petals joined to each other

Draw a buttercup flower

You might find a hand lens useful.

What's in a buttercup flower?

Pull off the five sepals.
These help to protect the flower.

Now detach the five petals.
The bright colour attracts insects.

Next, detach the anthers. These are made of filaments with pollen sacs at their tips.

Lastly, find the carpels at the centre of the flower.

Stick the different parts along a strip of Sellotape.

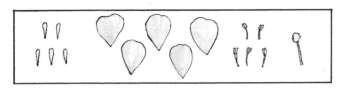

sepals   petals   stamens   carpels

Half flower

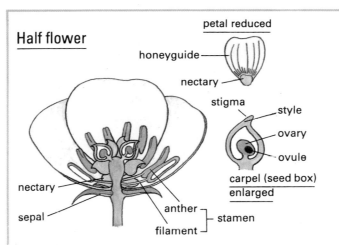

petal reduced
honeyguide
nectary
stigma
style
ovary
ovule
carpel (seed box)
enlarged
nectary
sepal
anther
filament
stamen

Exploded flower

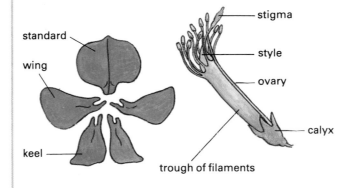

standard
wing
keel
stigma
style
ovary
calyx
trough of filaments

Whole flower (a collection of strap-shaped florets)

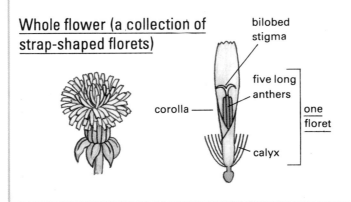

bilobed stigma
five long anthers
one floret
corolla
calyx

Meadow buttercup (*Ranunculaceae*)

calyx: outer ring of five green sepals

corolla: ring of five yellow petals (crown)

androecium: many pollen-producing stamens (male house)

gynaeceum: many carpels each producing a seed (female house)

Sweet pea (*Leguminosae*)

calyx: five green sepals

corolla: five petals, two anterior ones fused to form a 'keel', two 'wing' petals and a large posterior 'standard'

androecium: ten stamens, nine fused by their filaments to form a trough

gynaeceum: one carpel which forms the pea pod; the ovary inside contains a number of ovules which, when fertilised, become pea seeds

Dandelion (*Compositae*)

calyx: a pappus of hairs

corolla: five petals fused to form a long strap-shaped structure

androecium: five stamens

gynaeceum: two fused carpels containing one ovule

Insect search

In the summer term, see how many different types of insect you can find on flowers in the school garden. Try to identify them.

Make a chart of flowers and the insects visiting them.

Butterflies can be reared in an outdoor cage.

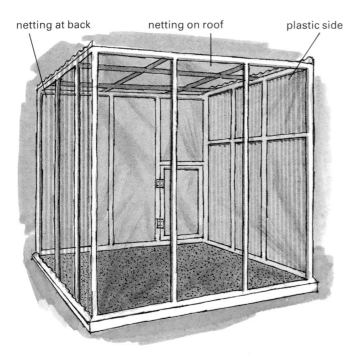

netting at back   netting on roof   plastic side

Ideas children can meet

Some flowers have nectar which insects like to feed on.
Nectar is a sweet liquid.
Bees make honey from nectar.
Some flowers smell nice and have bright petals: insects like these flowers.
Insects are important to some flowers because they carry pollen from flower to flower (pollination).

Make a garden for insects

cabbage white butterfly

buddleia or butterfly bush

cinnabar moth

red admiral butterfly

ragwort

honey bee

lavender

rose

nettle

bumble bee   hoverfly

michaelmas daisy

red clover

The composition of a rye-grass flower

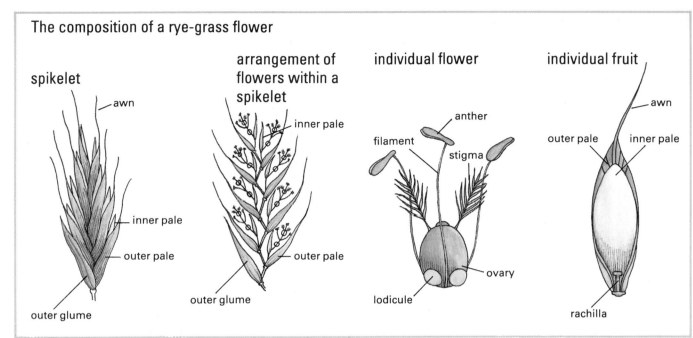

spikelet
- awn
- inner pale
- outer pale
- outer glume

arrangement of flowers within a spikelet
- inner pale
- outer pale
- outer glume

individual flower
- anther
- filament
- stigma
- ovary
- lodicule

individual fruit
- awn
- outer pale
- inner pale
- rachilla

Grass flowers are easily missed because they are so small and lack bright petals.

Make a grass collection

In the summer term, collect grasses from your school grounds or local park and identify them.

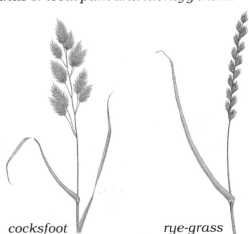

cocksfoot

rye-grass

couch grass

meadow grass

timothy

Press some grasses

Many grasses are easy to press, particularly the 'feathery' sorts.

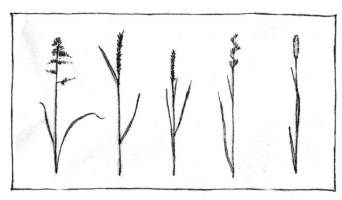

Make some large wall pictures by sticking grasses to card with sticky-backed plastic.

Grow some grasses

Plant the seeds in moistened potting compost and keep records.

Seed	Date	Age	Height
maize			
rye grass			

Ideas children can meet

Not all flowers smell nice and have pretty petals. Grasses have flowers too. Because they are wind pollinated, they do not need to have brightly coloured petals to attract insects.

Grasses produce masses of pollen. This is carried by the wind to other grasses and helps to make seeds.

Weeds are plants growing where people don't want them. A garden flower is a weed in a wheat field.

Draw some weeds

Dig up a common weed growing in the school grounds. Wash the roots and spread carefully on a paper towel.

Make a drawing of your weed. With most weeds you can make your drawing life-size.

Look at the parts of a weed

Flowers or fruit
Where are they?
What colour are they?
How are they arranged?

Stem
Is it round, square or ribbed?
Does it branch?
Is it hairy?
What colour is it?

Root
Does it vary in thickness?
Does it branch?
Is it hairy?
What colour is it?
Is it stiff, wirey, hard, woody, soft or slimy?

Leaves
What shape are they?
Are they hairy?
What colour are they?
Are they the same colour on the top and bottom?
Are the leaves in pairs or spirals?
Are there veins?
Where are the oldest leaves?
What is the leaf edge like?

Height and depth of weeds

Collect several common weeds from the school grounds. Measure their height above ground and their depth below it.

Make a chart.

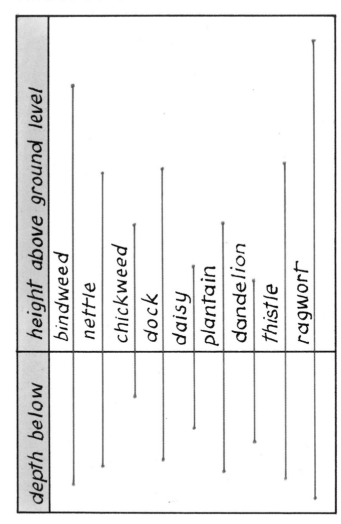

Annual weeds tend to have more shallow roots than perennials.

Variation in dandelion leaves

Do dandelions growing in different places have leaves of different sizes?

Look for leaves: on a lawn
in neglected long grass
among hedgerow plants
near footpaths
at the base of walls.

Press the leaves and mount them under sticky-backed plastic.

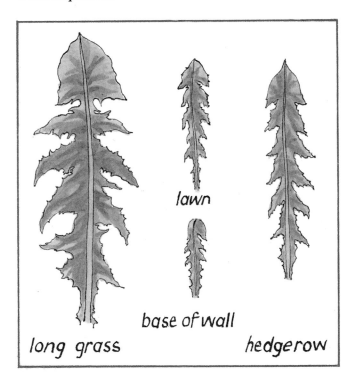

lawn

base of wall

long grass   hedgerow

Pulling up weeds

Measure, with a force meter, the force needed to pull up a weed.

Place a garden cane alongside a selected weed. Strap it to the weed with a piece of raffia to get a good purchase. Attach the meter to the end of the raffia and pull steadily.

How easy is it to pull up different species?
How easy is it to pull up different weeds of the same species?
Try altering the moisture of the soil. What happens?

	pull in dry soil			pull in wet soil		
	plant 1	plant 2	plant 3	plant 1	plant 2	plant 3
dock						
chickweed						
dandelion						

Colonization

Some weeds rapidly colonize cleared ground. Grasses and quickly-seeding garden weeds, such as chickweed, are usually the first to appear.

Clear a 2 metre square of ground and sieve the soil to remove all roots and other material.

Fence in the cleared area with chicken wire. After a month see what plants have grown. Keep a record over a six-month period and plot the plants to scale.

chickweed

groundsel   grass

Trampling

If your school has grassy areas used by children, you can find out the paths most frequently used.

matchsticks driven into the soil with not more than 1 cm protruding

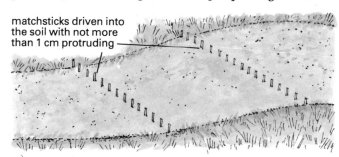

Drive in the matchsticks first thing in the morning and examine the path at the end of the school day. The most trampled paths have the most broken matchsticks.

These do not contain chlorophyll and thus, unlike most plants, they cannot make their own food. They live as saprophytes (on decaying material) or as parasites. They reproduce by spores.

Make a collection

Autumn is the best time for fungal forays. Children must wash their hands after touching fungi since many are poisonous.

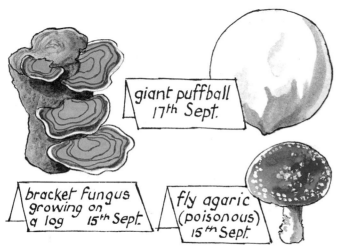

giant puffball 17th Sept.

bracket fungus growing on a log 15th Sept.

fly agaric (poisonous) 15th Sept.

Take some photographs

Sketch or paint

field mushroom (edible)

Make some spore prints

You need mature, fresh, gill-bearing fungi to make good prints. Cut off the stalk and put the cap, gills downwards, on to a sheet of white paper.

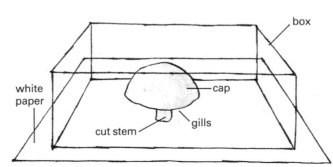

box

white paper

cap

cut stem

gills

Cover with a box to exclude draughts and leave overnight. The spores can be black, white, green, brown, purple, or pink depending on the species. The patterns formed vary from species to species.

Use this method if the spores fall off easily.

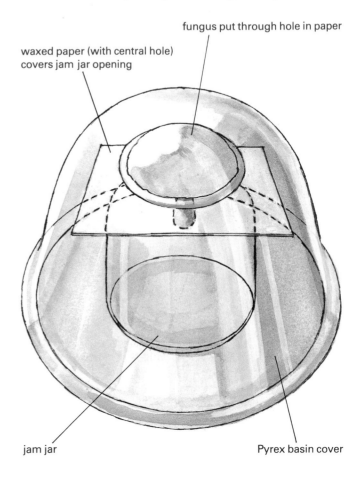

fungus put through hole in paper

waxed paper (with central hole) covers jam jar opening

jam jar

Pyrex basin cover

If the spores drop on to the waxed paper, you can make a permanent record by gently warming the paper so that the wax just melts. When it hardens you have a fixed spore print.

Ideas children can meet

Many fungi are poisonous.
Fungi do not have green leaves, but are still plants.
They can live on decaying things.
Fungi grow from spores.

Seaweeds belong to the group of plants called algae. They cling with a holdfast to rocks. Their structure is simple, consisting of fronds that form the plant body. There are four distinct groups: blue-green, green, brown and red algae. The blue-green algae are found around the high water mark. There is a gradation down the shore from this point, through the green and brown algae to the red, which are found in deep water. All contain chlorophyll. If you pour boiling water on the brown and red algae, the pigment oozes out, leaving the green chlorophyll in the frond.

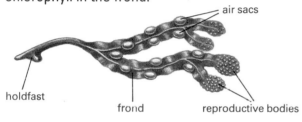

air sacs

holdfast

frond

reproductive bodies

Seaweeds will keep for about ten days in a bucket of salt water.

Looking at bladder-wrack

Bladder-wrack is one of the most common seaweeds on British shores and can often be found after winter storms, cast up on beaches.

What does it feel like?
What colour is it?
Does it have roots, stems or leaves?
How does it anchor itself to the rocks?
Try squeezing the 'bobbles'. What happens?

Pressing bladder-wrack

Tough, leathery seaweeds like bladder-wrack need special treatment before pressing.

Wash the seaweed well under a tap.

Then soak in hot water for an hour.

Press for a couple of weeks.

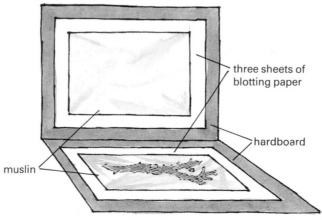

three sheets of blotting paper

hardboard

muslin

Mount with a strong adhesive.

Mounting delicate seaweeds

Delicate seaweeds, which are often red or green, can be floated out on paper in a bowl of seawater. Always use seawater, otherwise the colour may fade. Float and spread the weed carefully on the paper.

Cover the dried paper and weed with clear, sticky-backed plastic.

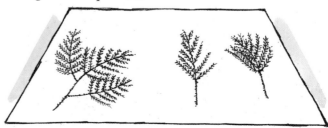

Even in towns, hedges can be found around parks or gardens, providing a habitat for small animals and plants. Hawthorn hedges are usually full of wildlife, while holly or beech are comparatively sterile. Privet hedges are common in towns.

The greater the variety of shrubs, the greater the variety of wildlife.

The best time to investigate a mature hedge is during the autumn but you could try a year-round hedge survey.

Although many hedges have been uprooted in the countryside in recent years, you can still find old field boundary hedges in all areas – even East Anglia. Some hedges in the countryside are very old and have a wide range of plants. Some have mature trees.

In some areas, such as Cornwall or Yorkshire, field boundaries are stone walls. These are rich in ferns, mosses and lichens. The crevices harbour slugs, snails, and lizards.

You will need

2 metre cane

secateurs

compass

clip-board

reel tape measure

polythene collecting bag

Which way does the hedge run?

Measure the height of the hedge,

How wide is the hedge at the bottom?

Make a list of the shrubs in the hedge.

Walk along a 10-metre length of the hedge and find out the most common shrub.

Make a list of any mature trees.

Take twigs from any shrubs or trees you cannot name, for future identification.

Make a collection of leaves from each kind of tree and shrub for later pressing, mounting and labelling.

Are there any fruits on the shrubs? What are they called? How are they dispersed?

Look for and identify climbing plants. Some scramble, some twine and some have tendrils.
What helps the scramblers to climb?
Which twiners curl in a clockwise direction? Which anticlockwise?

Look for mosses, fungi, lichens, liverworts and flowering plants.

Measure the shadow cast by the hedge. Does one side get more sun than the other?
Does this affect the kind of vegetation on each side of the hedge?
Does the prevailing wind affect the hedge?

Look for signs of animals, such as partly-eaten leaves, galls, spiders' webs, snails' shells or trails, footprints and nests.

Look for animals, such as hedgehogs, spiders and butterfly pupae.

Is there any rubbish in your hedge?

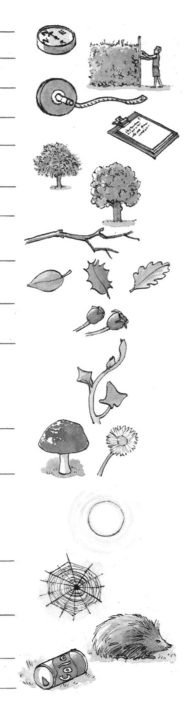

Measurement on a privet hedge

Pluck the leaves from about 100 privet twigs. Make groups of leaves 0–5 mm, 6–10 mm, 11–15 mm etc in length. Make a graph of your results.

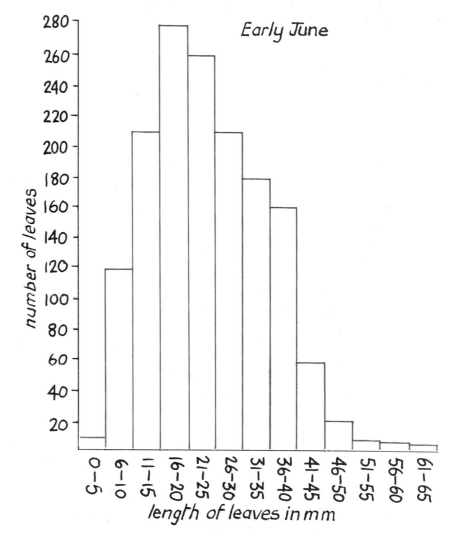

Early June

number of leaves / length of leaves in mm

Discuss the distribution by length. For example, few small and few large and many in the middle range.

Do plants give off water?

Tie a plastic bag over the end of a leafy twig.

Leave for 24 hours and see how much water collects on the inside of the bag.

Now do the same with a twig stripped of leaves. What happens?

Measure the water given off

Stand a weed (groundsel or shepherd's purse) in a jam jar and support it by a piece of card.

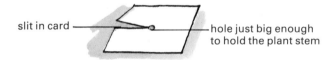

slit in card — hole just big enough to hold the plant stem

Set up a control jam jar with no weed.

What happens to the water level in each case? Why?
You could try different weeds to see which loses most or least water.
Try waxy leaves, such as holly, and compare with non-waxy leaves such as sycamore.

How does water get up to the leaves?

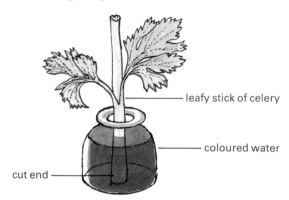

leafy stick of celery

coloured water

cut end

After a few days, cut across the stem and examine it with a hand lens.

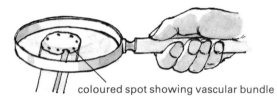

coloured spot showing vascular bundle

Make a red, white and blue flower

Split a white carnation stem lengthwise into three. Put one part into clear water, the others into red and blue solutions as shown below.

Leave for a day.

Make some orange daisies

Wash the roots free of soil first. Then place in water coloured with orange dye.

How much water?

Water makes up a large proportion of many living organisms.

Cut 100 g of potato into thin slices. Spread them on a baking sheet and dry over a radiator or in a warm oven for ten minutes.

Weigh them and record the result. Keep drying, weighing and recording at ten-minute intervals.

Graph the results.

You will get anything between a 50% and 80% water loss, depending on the efficiency of your drying method.

Ideas children can meet

Plants need water.
Leaves give off water.
Water travels up the stems and trunks of plants.
Water gets into the plants through the roots.
Roots get water from the soil.

Do pea roots grow towards water?

Plant soaked pea seeds in a light soil, mixed with sawdust. Arrange the seeds in a ring around a water-filled porous pot. When the shoots emerge, gently scrape the soil away from the seedlings.

soil and sawdust

In which direction are they growing?

Do the same experiment, leaving the porous pot dry and watering the soil only.

What happens. Why?

Do wheat seedlings grow towards the light?

Plant wheat seeds in two separate trays of soil. Put one out-of-doors where light falls from above.

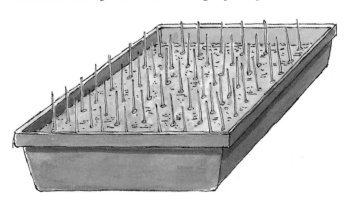

Put the other on a window-sill with light coming from one side only.

What happens. Why?

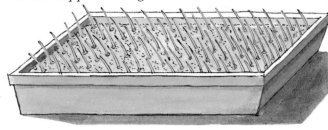

Do potato sprouts like light?

Make a potato maze from an old shoe box. Put a freshly sprouting potato at one end of your maze box.

Keep the lid on except for an occasional peek.

Do broad bean seedlings like the cold?

Select three similar seedlings. Put one on a warm window-sill which gets some sun, another in a cold shed, and the third in a refrigerator. Remember that the absence of light also affects the growth.

Keep the soil moist. Observe how each seedling grows.

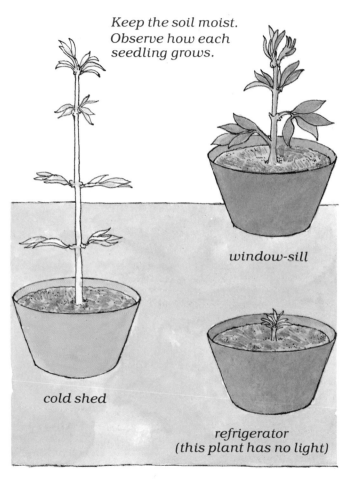

window-sill

cold shed

refrigerator
(this plant has no light)

Ideas children can meet

Plants show growth movements towards light and water.
Temperature also affects plant growth.

Look at: size
shape of body
shape of beak
shape of feet and legs
shape when flying.

Draw attention to a familiar yardstick when judging size.

As big as a sparrow.

As big as a blackbird.

As big as a pigeon.

Make bird silhouettes

Draw silhouettes of birds common to the school grounds on black sugar paper.
Draw them to scale, with chalk.
Cut them out and mount them on the windows.

Standing

Sparrow
Greenfinch
Pigeon
Wagtail
Robin
Starling
Blackbird
Thrush
Common gull
chaffinch
Great tit

Flying
Pigeon
Thrush
Starling
Great Tit
Greenfinch
Robin
Sparrow
wagtail
Common gull
Chaffinch
Blackbird

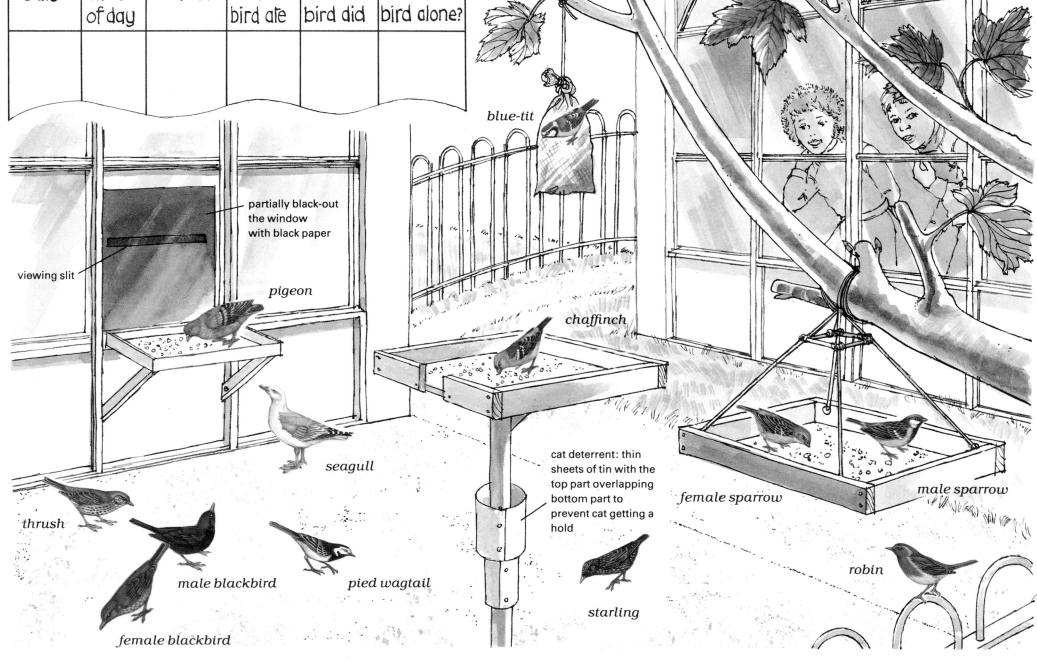

Date	Time of day	Weather	What the bird ate	What the bird did	Was the bird alone?

viewing slit

partially black-out the window with black paper

pigeon

blue-tit

chaffinch

seagull

thrush

male blackbird

pied wagtail

female blackbird

cat deterrent: thin sheets of tin with the top part overlapping bottom part to prevent cat getting a hold

starling

female sparrow

male sparrow

robin

male

female

How many males and females in the playground?

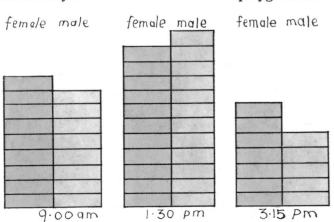

Watch sparrows feeding

How does a sparrow feed? Does it hold the food down to peck at it?

What is the biggest piece of bread a sparrow will fly off with?

What colours do sparrows like?

Food colouring is not harmful to sparrows. Dye lightly-cooked rice with different colours. Which is the favourite?

When do sparrows feed?

Watch the feeding table at regular intervals throughout the day. Make a spot check every 15 or 30 minutes.

Graph your results.

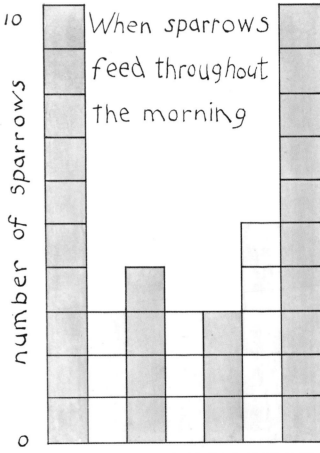

Usually the birds feed heavily first thing in the morning with a peak around noon and a final feeding phase towards the end of the day. This is particularly true in cold weather.

Watch sparrows moving

Scatter some breadcrumbs on the ground to attract sparrows.

Place a metre rule on the ground.

Watch the sparrows from a distance. Can you judge the length of each hop?

Watch sparrows flying.

Their flight is a short flap and then a glide so that they seem to move in darts.

Weigh a sparrow

Use a spring balance capable of weighing up to 100 grams. You should be able to read the scale from the classroom window, using binoculars.

The small bag of peanuts should not have a mass of more than 50 grams. It is easier to calculate the mass of the bird if you have exactly 50 grams of peanuts in the bag.

Make a sparrow book

Include details of experiments as well as information on habits etc. You could collect feathers and pictures from magazines too.

Which colours do birds like?

Some birds, such as tits, love peanuts, especially during the winter. Use unshelled nuts and paint the shells different colours. Water-based poster paints, thinly spread, are the best. Don't use oil-based paints.

Fix the peanuts to a length of tape with needle and thread. Include a few unpainted shells as a control.

Watch the birds visiting the nuts.

Which nuts do the birds go for? Keep a record.

Red	Blue	Yellow	Brown	Green	Orange	Normal
✓✓✓	✓		✓		✓	✓✓

Is there a favourite colour?
Do tits and sparrows go for the same colour?
How about other birds?

Collecting and cleaning nests

Collect nests in the autumn and winter, never during the brood-raising months.

Wear gloves when handling nests and place in a garden shed to dry. When dry, put your nest in a large polythene bag and dust it with a pyrethrum insecticide. Leave for a few days.

Children can now touch the nests but should always wash their hands afterwards.

Investigating a nest

Draw the nest. Weigh it. Measure it.

Take the nest to pieces, using fingers and tweezers. Separate the materials into different piles. Twigs, dried grass, moss, mud, feathers, even Sellotape and string may feature. Make a display sheet of your results.

Robin's nest
Mass of nest = 56g
Materials used
lining of hair | leaves and feathers | dried grass | moss

Beaks

House sparrow — Stumpy beak for eating seeds and insects.

Robin — Slender beak feeding on slugs, worms, insects, soft fruit, berries.

Starling — Chisel like beak, feeds on worms, snails, insects, spiders, fruit.

Thrush — Snails, worms, caterpillars, spiders, insects, berries.

Blackbird — Similar diet to the thrush.

Kestrel — Hooked tip. Insects, rodents, frogs, small birds.

Blue-tit — Insects, buds, seeds.

Mallard — Plants, insects, worms, small shell-fish.

Feet

Sparrow — Hopping

Hen — Scratching

Mallard — Swimming

Hawk — Catching prey

Moorhen — Walking

Woodpecker — Climbing

Wings

Eagle

Pheasant

Swallow — pointed

Warbler — rounded wings

Tails

Swallow — Forked

Starling — Short and square ended

Gull — Fan like

Pheasant — Long and pointed

Raven — Wedge shaped

Wagtail — Long and pointed. Wags up and down.

Watch water birds moving and feeding

Moorhens run along the surface of the water in order to take off, while teal jump straight out of the water.

moorhen

teal

Mallards up-end to search for seeds and water plants.

Coots dive straight in.

Tufted ducks jump before diving in open water.

Diving birds

Coots, tufted ducks and great crested grebes are among the water birds which dive under the water to search for food. Coots and tufted ducks will feed mainly on plants, grebe eat fish.

Use a stop-watch to time how long a bird stays underneath the water.

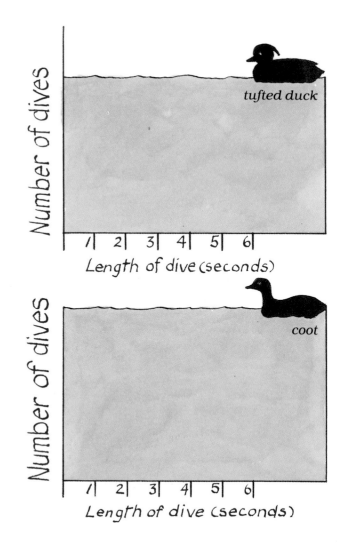

tufted duck

Number of dives

/1 2| 3| 4| 5| 6|
Length of dive (seconds)

coot

Number of dives

/1 2| 3| 4| 5| 6|
Length of dive (seconds)

tufted duck

mallard coming in to land

young mute swan (cygnet)

moorhen
(tail held high)

female mallard

male mallard

coot (tail held low)

pied wagtail

mute swan

Look for spiders in corners and cracks in walls, in the nooks and crannies of sheds and among plants. There are several types of spider living in houses. September is the best time for a spider search.

Keeping spiders

You can keep spiders for a few days for observation in small jars or clear plastic boxes.

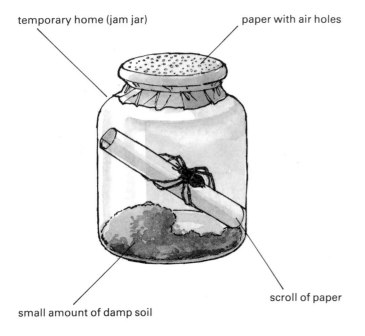

temporary home (jam jar)

paper with air holes

scroll of paper

small amount of damp soil

You must provide a bigger home if you want the spider to spin a web. Measure the size of its web outdoors to find out how large the cage should be.

Keep the spiders separate or they may eat each other. The cages should not be in bright sunlight since spiders like damp, cool conditions. Do not keep the spiders for more than a few days, unless you know what they eat. You can feed fly-eating spiders on small flies but many spiders feed on ants or woodlice or even small spiders.

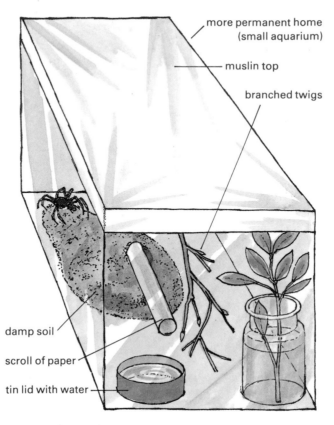

more permanent home (small aquarium)

muslin top

branched twigs

damp soil

scroll of paper

tin lid with water

Looking at a spider

Watch your spider for some time. The larger house spiders are best for observation but some of these can bite.

Make a drawing

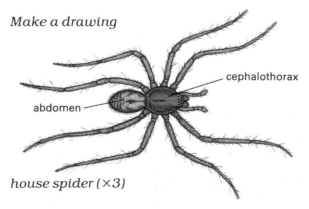

cephalothorax

abdomen

house spider (×3)

Hunt the webs

Look at the webs and draw them but don't destroy them. Go on a web hunt in the school grounds. Foggy autumn mornings are the best time. Newly made webs will be pristine.

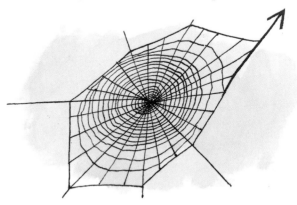

Used webs show holes, repaired places, flies in store and a strong communication line because of the frequent journeys by the spider.

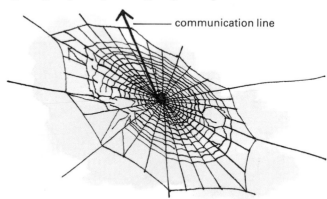

communication line

Some spiders spin hammock webs.

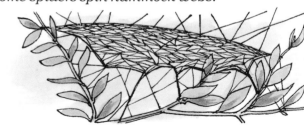

Web making

The garden spider takes only half an hour to make its orb-web. If you are lucky, and very quiet, you might see your captive spider building one.

First the spider makes a framework.

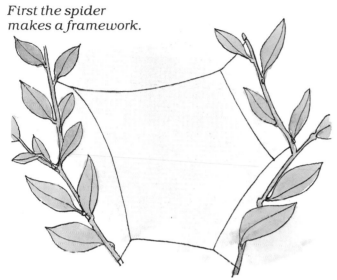

Then it builds spokes.

Next it makes a spiral of very thin thread from the middle to the outside. This is the initial scaffold.

The web is finished by a spiral from the outside to the middle, usually in a clockwise direction.

Sometimes spiders cast web threads in the air. Air currents determine where the thread falls. If it lands on a suitable object, the spider runs up the thread bridge and makes its web. Alternatively, a spider may fix a thread to a suitable support and then run across vegetation to attach the thread to a second support. With both ends secured, web-building begins.

Look for spider cocoons

You can find these between leaves or under stones. The young eventually emerge, using parachutes of silken thread.

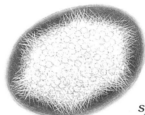

spider cocoon (×4)

Dangling

Put a spider on the end of a stick. Shake it gently.

Watch it fall on its silken thread.
Does it fall far?
Watch it climb back up the thread.
Which legs does it use?
What happens to the thread?

Moulting

Look for cast skins left in ledges. You should be able to mount a series of skins from about 5 to 40 mm in length.

There are many species of stick insect. The one most commonly kept in schools is *Carausius morosus*. All are females; males are known but are extremely rare. The females reproduce by parthenogenesis. Stick insects are wingless, active by night and are nocturnal feeders. Their food is plant material, usually privet. They will also eat ivy, polyanthus and holly. There are three stages in the life history of a stick insect: egg, nymph (miniature adult) and adult.

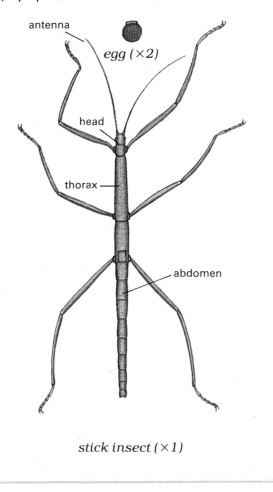

antenna

egg (×2)

head

thorax

abdomen

stick insect (×1)

Keeping stick insects

The young nymphs can be kept in a glass jam jar, and fed on tender privet leaves.

Use a camel-haired brush to transfer the young nymphs. Newly-hatched stick insects are very thirsty so provide them with some moistened cotton wool.

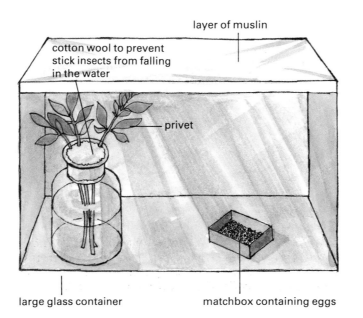

layer of muslin

cotton wool to prevent stick insects from falling in the water

privet

large glass container

matchbox containing eggs

Playing dead

This attitude is the normal daytime one. Draw a motionless death-feigning stick insect.

Stick insects often fall to the bottom of their cage and lie motionless in the death-feigning attitude.

Try warming an insect in this state in the palm of your hand. What happens?

Watch stick insects feeding

Look at a leaf which has been nibbled by a stick insect.

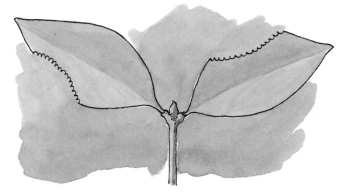

The biting mouthparts (mandibles) work sideways. The small 'bites' which result can easily be seen.

Make an outline drawing of a twig on a squared paper. This can be compared with the eaten twig on successive days.

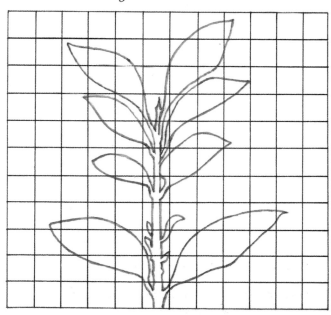

Measure growth

A stick insect moults continually throughout its life. At each moult it increases in length by about 25%.

Measure the length at each successive moult.

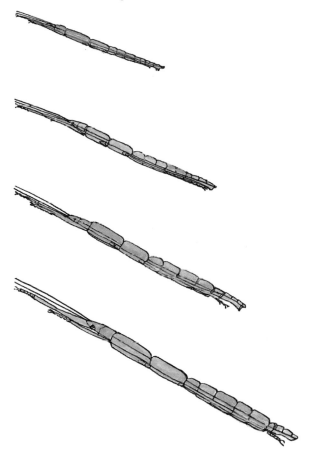

Camouflage

Stick insects use their shape, colour and attitude to mimic twigs. Colour varies from green to brown and the animals can move pigment in and out of their surface cells, thus making them darker or paler.

Make some small drawings of stick insects and colour them with a variety of shades. Cut them out carefully and put them on a privet twig.

How good is the camouflage?
How many can other people spot?

Looking at eggs

The oval eggs are brown or black, with a lid at one end where the nymph escapes. The eggs are well camouflaged when among seeds.

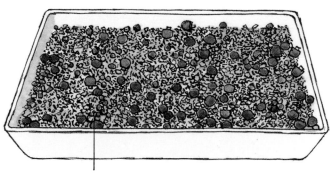

mixture of seeds and stick insect eggs

Put a fixed number of eggs into mixed seeds. Who can find most eggs in one minute?

How to keep caterpillars

The cabbage white is found in most vegetable gardens, where it lays its eggs on plants of the cabbage family. They are easy to keep as their food plant is common.

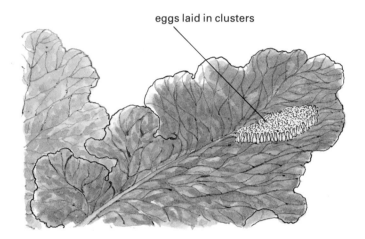

eggs laid in clusters

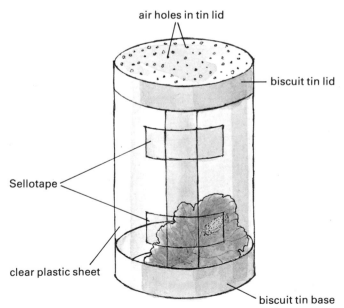

air holes in tin lid

biscuit tin lid

Sellotape

clear plastic sheet

biscuit tin base

Keep the eggs until they hatch.

Transfer the newly-hatched caterpillar, using a paintbrush.

Put the caterpillars in an old aquarium with plenty of food. They will get their water from the leaves so there is no need to provide water separately. You must, however, change the plant food daily.

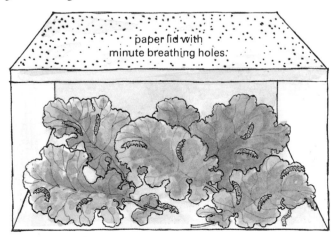

paper lid with minute breathing holes

Try keeping caterpillars of other species, provided that you have a plentiful supply of their food plant.

Looking at caterpillars

Draw an egg, using a hand lens for greater detail.

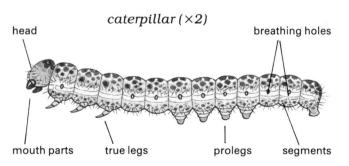

egg (×50)

Using a hand lens, draw a caterpillar.

caterpillar (×2)

head

breathing holes

mouth parts   true legs   prolegs   segments

How long?
What colour?
Hairy or smooth?
How many segments?
How many legs?
How many breathing holes?

How does a caterpillar eat?
Does it tear at the leaf?
Does it eat quickly?

How much does a caterpillar eat?

Put your caterpillar in a separate container with a leaf of its food plant.

Make a record of the leaf at the start of each day.

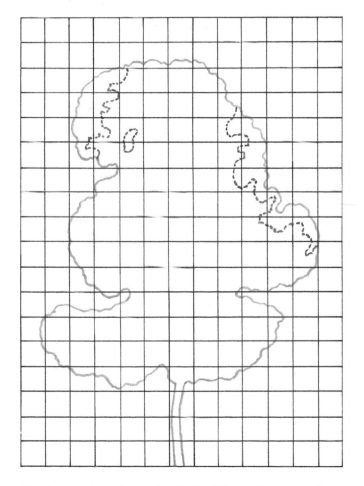

Next morning show, by dotted lines, how much has been eaten.

Keep growth records

Do caterpillars grow steadily or in spurts?
Measure their length each day.

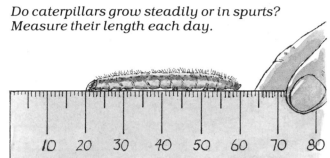

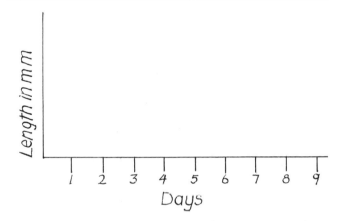

Watch a caterpillar moving

How does it move?
How fast does it move?

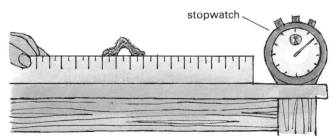

What does the caterpillar do when it gets to the end of the ruler?

Make a life cycle wheel

hole for
paper fastener

THE BUTTERFLY LIFECYCLE

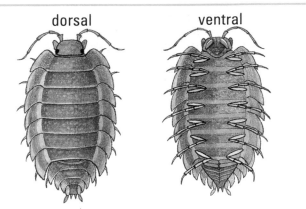

dorsal ventral

Woodlice are common under stones, in damp sheds and beneath rotting logs. They belong to the same group as crabs and lobsters, but woodlice are the only crustaceans to have conquered the land. Females have a small pouch on their undersides. Eggs are laid at the beginning of summer and hatch after about five weeks. The young then leave the mother. Woodlice moult from time to time as they grow.

Looking at woodlice

Using a hand lens, draw a woodlouse.
How many legs?
What colour?
Is it hairy?
How long?

woodlouse (×2)

old covering falling off

Can you find a moulting woodlouse?

Keeping woodlice

Woodlice are easy to keep. The container should be in a shady place, with moss to keep the soil damp. Clean the container every three weeks.

paper with breathing holes

moss

piece of rotting wood

pieces of potato

pieces of chalk help to make their outer covering hard

rock

damp soil

One type of woodlouse, the common pill bug, rolls up when you touch it.

Watch woodlice feeding

What do they eat? Try chopped potato, carrot, turnip, lettuce, tiny pieces of meat. Woodlice in the wild often feed on decaying leaves.

Woodlice feed mostly at night. Try turning night into day by keeping them illuminated at night and covered up during the day.

When do they move about more?
When do they rest?

Warning: do not let the woodlice get too hot under illumination.

Wet or dry: dark or light?

Use a shallow tray (take-away food container). Keep one half of the tray damp and the other half dry.

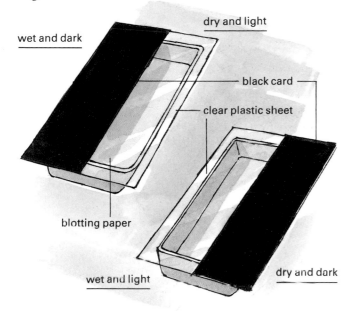

wet and dark
dry and light
black card
clear plastic sheet
blotting paper
wet and light
dry and dark

Place ten woodlice in the centre of each tray. Fifteen minutes later, count how many are in each half.

Choice	Number of woodlice						
	1st try	2nd try	3rd try	4th try	5th try	Total	Average
wet and dark							
wet and light							
dry and dark							
dry and light							

Looking at colour

Make a chequerboard grid of 16 squares.

Place the chequerboard in a steep-sided bowl or tray.

Put one woodlouse on each square. Where are they ten minutes later? Check every ten minutes for the next hour.

Which way for dinner?

Make a simple T-junction maze from an old shirt box.

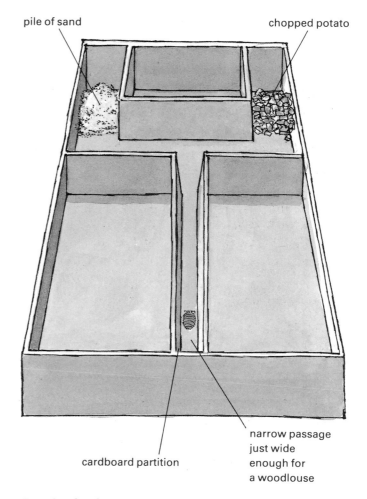

pile of sand
chopped potato
narrow passage just wide enough for a woodlouse
cardboard partition

Put the food in one corner and make a sandy desert in the other.

Can you 'train' your woodlouse to turn one way?

Snails live in damp places, such as under stones, among plants or in crevices in walls. They move about in wet weather, leaving a slime trail. The slime helps them to cling and reduces friction on rough surfaces. When it is very cold or dry, snails seal themselves into their shells by producing a slime which hardens over the entrance to their shell. They hibernate by the same means. Snails feed on plants by rasping away at them with a long file-like tongue called a radula. Snail eggs are laid in clusters in damp soil.

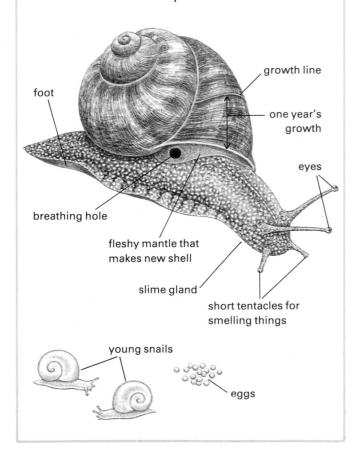

foot
growth line
one year's growth
eyes
breathing hole
fleshy mantle that makes new shell
slime gland
short tentacles for smelling things
young snails
eggs

Keeping snails

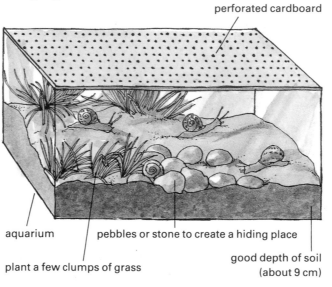

perforated cardboard
aquarium
plant a few clumps of grass
pebbles or stone to create a hiding place
good depth of soil (about 9 cm)

Feed the snails on cabbage, lettuce, mashed potato and flour paste. Add fresh food every day and clear out any stale bits. Clean the container every three weeks.

Look for eggs just below the surface of the soil. Put them in a small jam jar of soil, covered by a polythene bag pricked with air holes.

Draw a snail

Looking at the shell

What colour?
How tall?
How wide?
How old?
Hard or soft?
Which way does it spiral?

When a snail dies, its soft body decays leaving the shell intact.

Rubbing down a snail's shell on sandpaper will eventually expose the internal structure.

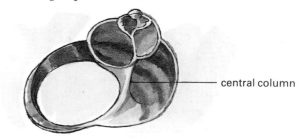

central column

The snail is attached to its shell's central column by a strong muscle.

Watching snails move

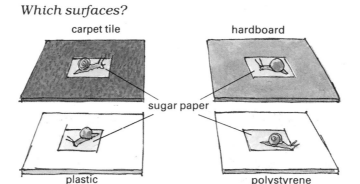

How fast?

Will a snail climb over obstacles?

Watch the muscular foot move.

You can see the muscles as grey rippling bands. How many can you count?

Which surfaces?

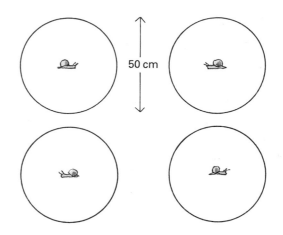

carpet tile

hardboard

sugar paper

plastic

polystyrene

Try glass, sandpaper and other surfaces. Which won't the snails cross?

Looking at snail trails

Put the snail in a deep tray and leave overnight.

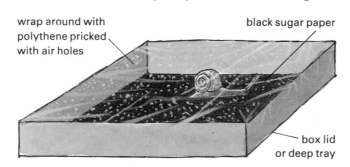

wrap around with polythene pricked with air holes

black sugar paper

box lid or deep tray

Look at the slime trail next morning and measure its length with string.

How well can snails see?

Bring a pencil slowly and carefully near its eyes.

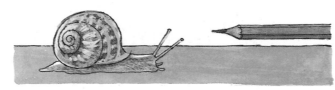

How close can you get before it withdraws its tentacles?

Snail races

Draw some circles (50 cm diameter) on paper. Place a snail at the centre of each circle.

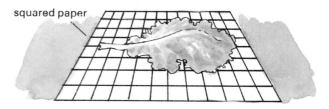

50 cm

Which one crawls out of the circle first? How long does it take?

How much does a snail eat?

squared paper

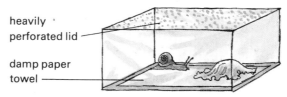

Draw around your leaf. Put the leaf in a box with a snail and leave it for 24 hours.

heavily perforated lid

damp paper towel

Remove the leaf. How much has been eaten? Do snails eat more of some leaves than others? Do they eat more if kept in the dark all the time? Do they eat more if kept in a warm place?

There are a number of British species of earthworm. Identification is difficult because many small worms may just be immature specimens of larger ones. The largest species, *Lumbricus terrestris* , is 90–300 mm in length with 110–160 segments.

It is a commonly held belief that earthworms can regenerate parts if they are cut in two, but this is difficult for many species – *Lumbricus terrestris* is an example. *Eisenia foetida*, commonly found in compost heaps, can regenerate more easily. Earthworms are active at night, using body muscles and bristles to push their way through the soil. They move deeper into the soil in dry weather. Dig for worms where you find casts on the soil surface. A warm evening after rain is the best time and be prepared to go down 300–400 mm.

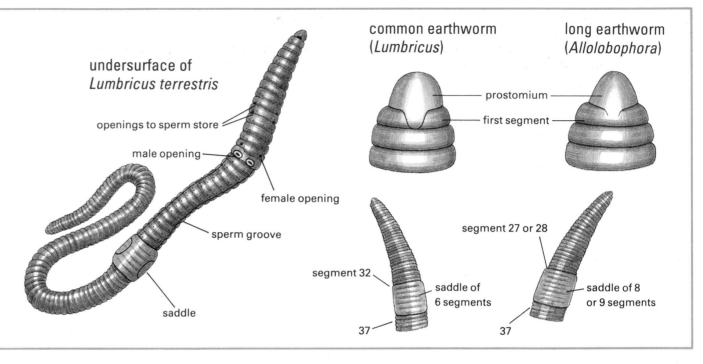

undersurface of *Lumbricus terrestris*

openings to sperm store

male opening

female opening

sperm groove

saddle

common earthworm (*Lumbricus*)

long earthworm (*Allolobophora*)

prostomium

first segment

segment 27 or 28

segment 32

saddle of 6 segments

saddle of 8 or 9 segments

37

37

Looking at worms

Study a worm carefully, using a hand lens for further detail.

Try modelling a worm in Plasticine.

Keeping worms in wormeries

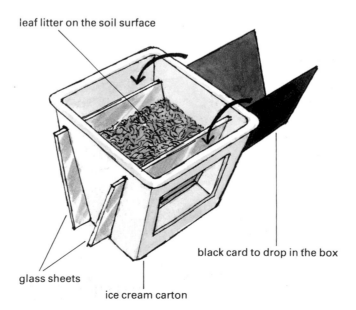

leaf litter on the soil surface

black card to drop in the box

glass sheets

ice cream carton

Use a mixture of garden loam and Levington Compost to fill each wormery. Do not water the mixture in the wormery as this destroys the soil structure. Moisten the soil before putting it in the wormery and test it by squeezing it in your hand to see if the crumb structure holds together. Wormeries are best kept out of doors.

You can make a more simple wormery from an old squash bottle.

cut down squash bottle

black sugar paper sleeve

Worms that become too dry, or are subject to constant vibrations, or are kept in strong light will refuse to perform. If you want action, bear this in mind and use fresh worms for each test.

Little and large

Try using a piece of cotton to measure the length of a worm when it is at its longest and shortest.

Crossing gaps

Will worms cross gaps?
Start with a small gap between some books.
Repeat the tests and increase the distance between the books each time.

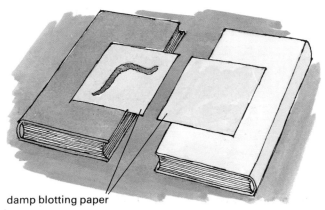

damp blotting paper

Light or dark?

Place several worms at the centre of a bowl, on some damp paper. Shine a lamp on to the exposed half.

How noisy?

Hold a sheet of brown paper, on which a worm is lying, close to your ear. You should be able to hear the bristles (chaetae) scratching on the paper as the worm moves.

Film show

Watch the worms moving and make a 'flick' book to show a worm crawling across a surface. Can you make it wriggle?

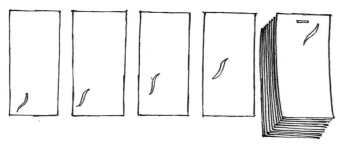

Wet or dry?

Place several worms at the centre of a bowl. One side should have damp newspaper, the other dry newspaper. Cover to keep out the light.

Where are the worms after five minutes? Repeat at least three times with fresh worms each time.

dry newspaper

damp newspaper

There are three species of frog in Britain: *Rana esculenta* (the edible frog), *Rana temporaria* (the common frog) and *Rana ridibuna* (the marsh frog). The common frog is the only true native species. *Bufo bufo*, the common toad, and *Bufo calamita*, the natterjack toad, are the two British toads. Both frogs and toads are found in damp places. They both move about at night and hide during the day under stones or in holes. Females are always bigger than males. Any frog over 5 cm is almost certainly a female, as is any toad over 6.5 cm.

Frogs

More agile than toads and progress by leaps.
Moist appearance and moist to the touch.
Feet more webbed than a toad's feet because frogs are more aquatic.
Pronounced typanum (ear drum) just behind each eye.
Teeth in upper jaw.
No neck glands.

Toads

Lumbering walk, with clumsy hops.
Dry, rough skin and dry feel.
Webbed feet.
Typanum much less pronounced.
No teeth.
Two large neck (parotid) glands on each side of the neck. These produce venom, harmless to people.

common frog
(4–8 cm)

frog spawn

common toad
(6–8 cm)

toad spawn

Keeping frogs and toads

Keep frogs and toads for observation for a few days only. They need plenty of space and moist surroundings. The container (an old aquarium will do) should be kept in the shade.

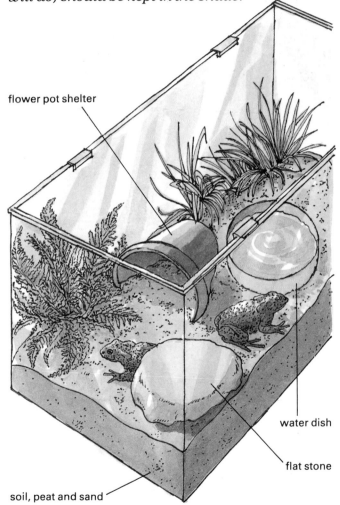

flower pot shelter

water dish

flat stone

soil, peat and sand

Feed them on worms, slugs, mealworms, gentles (the larvae of bluebottle flies) and insects. If they don't settle down, release them in suitable surroundings.

Watch them breathing

Frogs and toads breathe through their moist skin and by gulping air. Watch the throat movements as the animal pushes air into its lungs.

Count the number of gulps a minute at rest. Count again after the animal has been moving around.

Changing colour

Frogs can move the pigment (melanin) in their skins to become lighter or darker and thus match their surroundings.

Take two frogs of the same shade. Put one on a light background and the other on a dark background.

Remove them from these backgrounds and compare their colour after about 15 minutes. How long does it take for their skins to become the same colour?

From egg to frog

Keep tadpoles and watch their transition into frogs.

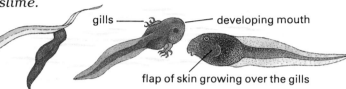

jelly

yolk

The newly-hatched tadpole clings to weed with slime.

gills — developing mouth

flap of skin growing over the gills

The tadpole starts to eat small animals as well as plants.

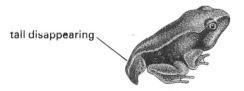

back legs emerging

The tadpole comes to the surface to breathe.

front legs emerging

The small frog leaves the water in June/July.

tail disappearing

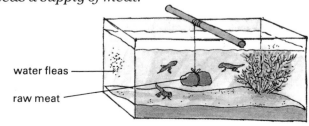

Once the tadpole has changed to a carnivore, it needs a supply of meat.

water fleas

raw meat

Keeping goldfish

Goldfish are inexpensive, hardy and easy to keep in school. An iron framed tank (60 cm × 30 cm × 30 cm) will house up to four fish of length 7–8 cm. Place the tank on a north-facing window-sill with the main light falling on the top of the tank. The back of the tank can be shaded. Tanks in direct sunlight overheat, lose oxygen and have overgrowths of algae. Set up the tank in situ since it can weigh up to 90 kg when full. Put in the sand and a rock or two, avoiding limestone and gypsum, which are soft and lose particles to the water. Run in the water, breaking the fall with a saucer.

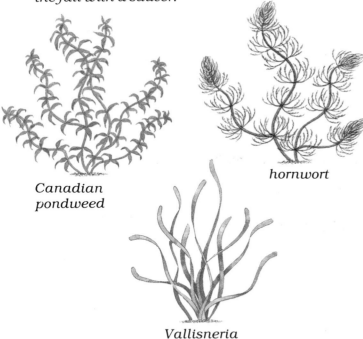

Canadian pondweed

hornwort

Vallisneria

Suitable plants are Canadian pondweed (Elodea canadensis), hornwort (Ceratophyllum species) and a grass-like plant Vallisneria spiralis, all available from garden centres. Plant 5–8 cm apart and weight if necessary. Leave the tank for about three weeks so that they can root firmly and the sand has time to pack down.

Siphon off one-third of the water each week and top up with water at much the same temperature as that already in the tank.

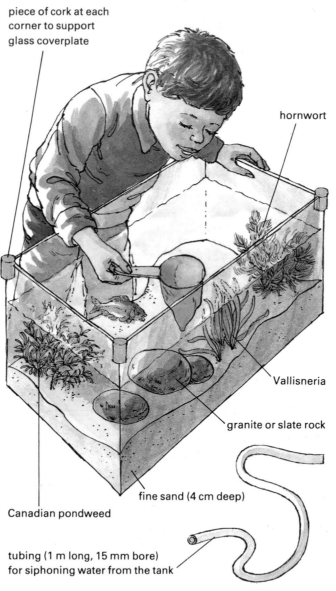

piece of cork at each corner to support glass coverplate

hornwort

Vallisneria

granite or slate rock

fine sand (4 cm deep)

Canadian pondweed

tubing (1 m long, 15 mm bore) for siphoning water from the tank

Feed your goldfish on proprietory foods, small earthworms, daphnia and tubiflex.

How does a goldfish swim?

Watch a goldfish swimming for five minutes. Which fins does it use?

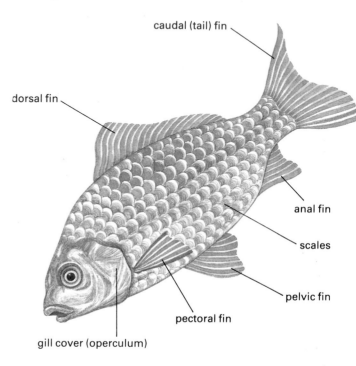

caudal (tail) fin

dorsal fin

anal fin

scales

pelvic fin

pectoral fin

gill cover (operculum)

Make a table like the one shown below.

Record the movements of the fins by placing a tick for each movement in the appropriate box.

pectoral	pelvic	tail	dorsal	anal
✓		✓✓		✓

The dorsal and anal fins act as stabilisers. The pectoral and pelvic fins adjust balance and are used to elevate the fish or to make it descend. The main propulsive force comes from the tail fin, which also acts as a rudder.

Watch a goldfish breathing

number of times open per minute			
fish still		fish just stopped moving rapidly	
mouth	gills	mouth	gills
✓	✓	✓✓	✓✓

The results should show a more rapid breathing rate after exercise, with the need to take up more oxygen.

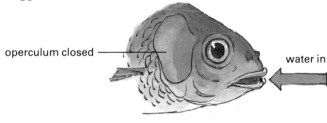

operculum closed — water in

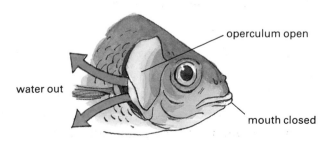

operculum open

water out — mouth closed

Fish breathe by taking in water through the mouth and passing it over the gills. Oxygen in the water is taken up by the gills.

Watch goldfish in a pond

How do the fish swim?
Do they swim in straight lines or in a zigzag way?
Watch the tail fin lashing from side to side.

Fish are very muscular and swim using the whole body, with tail and head leading the movements.

How old is a fish?

Fish scales have ring-like marks on them. These show up particularly well on a herring.

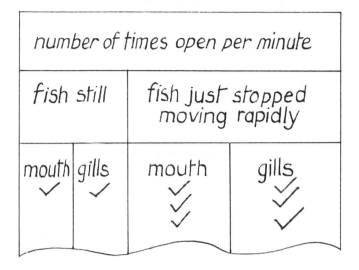

third winter

growth rings wider in the summer

second winter

first winter

part of scale embedded in the flesh

Why are ring widths different in summer from winter?

Draw a plaice

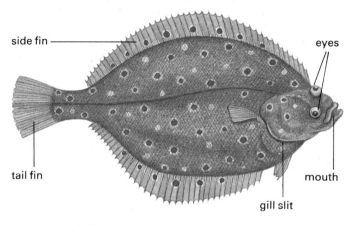

side fin

eyes

tail fin

mouth

gill slit

How is it different from a goldfish?

Think of: eyes
fins
shape
colour

These are all adaptations to life on the seabed.

Hide the fish

Make some paper plaice to merge with different coloured backgrounds.

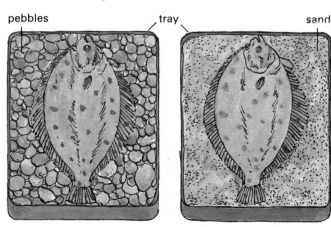

pebbles

tray

sand

Ponds are exciting places for children since they contain plants and animals outside children's normal experience. Animals and plants in ponds are specially adapted to their environment. The higher density of water means that water plants do not need as much supportive tissue as land plants. Also, the environment is fairly constant. Temperature does not fluctuate greatly and plants and animals do not suffer from desiccation.

Animals usually need to develop special means of breathing. Some have gills, such as dragonfly larvae, newts and fish. Others take bubbles of air down with them, for example *Corixa* (the water boatman). Locomotion in various pond animals is fascinating to watch: the long legs of pond-skaters skim over the surface, the limbs of the water boatman are like oars, and fish swim with sinuous movements.

Collecting equipment

sweep net   old metal tea strainer

pipettes

polythene bags   spoons

bucket   white pie dish

Take your catch back quickly. Polythene bags with a little water and lots of air space are best for transporting animals.

How and where to collect

Put a little pond water in the bottom of an old pie dish. Wade into the shallow regions of the pond, trying not to disturb the mud, and make some sweeps with the net. Gently tip the net into the dish, turn it inside out and rinse. Let the water settle for a minute or two. Examine for animals. Use a spoon (or pipette for very small organisms) to transfer any animal you want to a polythene bag containing water. Leave lots of air space when you tie the bag.

Use a metal tea strainer or flour sieve to collect mud samples from the pond floor. Wash this mud carefully to reveal segmented worms and blood worms (the larvae of two-winged flies).

Turn over stones slowly and carefully. Replace them just as carefully.

Look for flatworms between the overlapping bases of the rushes.

Keeping pond animals

Carnivorous animals should be housed separately from herbivorous ones.

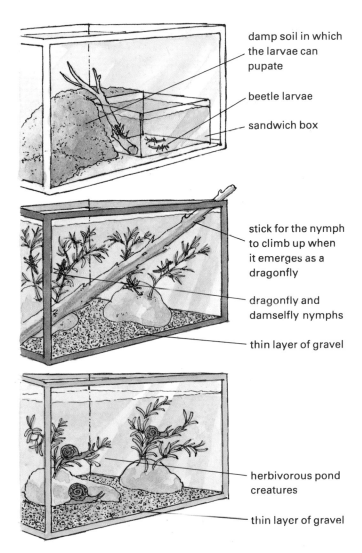

damp soil in which the larvae can pupate

beetle larvae

sandwich box

stick for the nymph to climb up when it emerges as a dragonfly

dragonfly and damselfly nymphs

thin layer of gravel

herbivorous pond creatures

thin layer of gravel

The carnivores can be fed on small segmented worms, water fleas and ant pupae (from pet shops). The herbivores will feed on the vegetation.

Sorting animals *Use keys to identify them.*

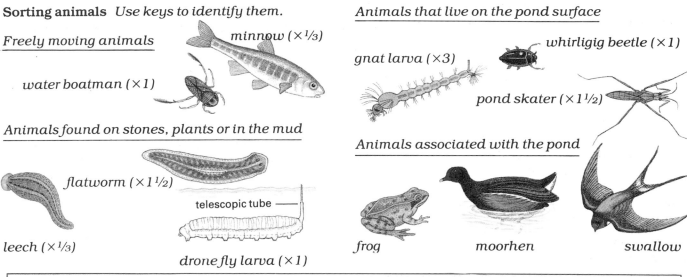

Freely moving animals

minnow (×⅓)

water boatman (×1)

Animals found on stones, plants or in the mud

flatworm (×1½)

leech (×⅓)

telescopic tube

drone fly larva (×1)

Animals that live on the pond surface

gnat larva (×3)

whirligig beetle (×1)

pond skater (×1½)

Animals associated with the pond

frog   moorhen   swallow

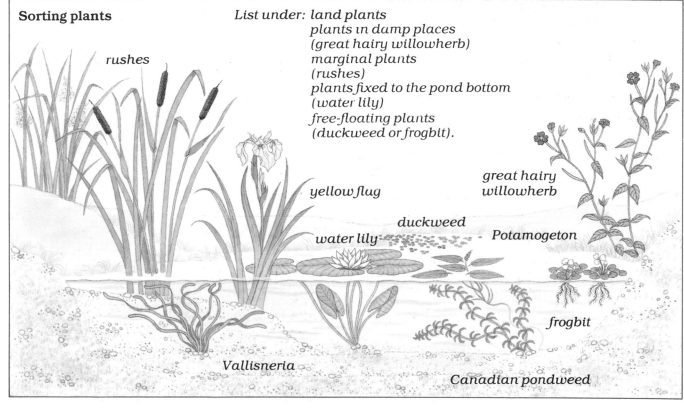

Sorting plants

List under: land plants
plants in damp places
(great hairy willowherb)
marginal plants
(rushes)
plants fixed to the pond bottom
(water lily)
free-floating plants
(duckweed or frogbit).

rushes

yellow flag

great hairy willowherb

duckweed

water lily

Potamogeton

Vallisneria

frogbit

Canadian pondweed

Pond animals: some basic questions

What colour is it?
How many parts are there to the body?
Does it have wings or wing covers?
How many legs and what are they like?
What are its eyes like?
How does it move?
How does it feed?
What does it feed on?
How does it breathe?
How does it reproduce?
What kind of life cycle does it have?

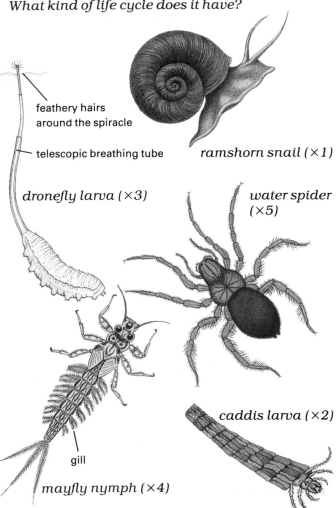

feathery hairs
around the spiracle

telescopic breathing tube

ramshorn snail (×1)

dronefly larva (×3)

water spider (×5)

caddis larva (×2)

gill

mayfly nymph (×4)

Many pond plants reproduce vegetatively. Two interesting ones for experiment are duckweed and Canadian pondweed.

Looking at duckweed

warm sunny window-sill

cool place in the classroom

Float one duckweed plant on pond-water in a jam jar. Put it on a sunny window-sill. Set up a second jar, but put this in a cool place.
Check how many duckweed plants there are in each jar, week by week.

Remember to keep the jars topped up with water.

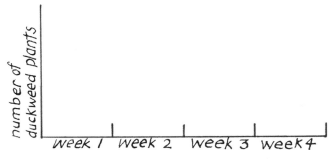

number of duckweed plants

week 1   week 2   week 3   week 4

Keep a separate graph (bar chart) for each jar.

Looking at Canadian pondweed

length 1cm
date 7 MAY

Length 2 cm
date 7 MAY

length 3 cm
date 7 MAY

length 4 cm
date 7MAY

length 5cm
date 7 MAY

Cut the leafy tips from five shoots of Canadian pondweed. Make them 1 cm, 2 cm, 3 cm, 4 cm and 5 cm in length, always making sure that you include the growing tip. Put each in a separate jar and label it with the date and length.
Keep the plants for a month and look at them weekly to see what happens. Measure them at the end of the month.

Response to light

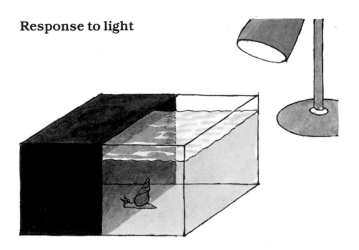

Half fill a plastic container with pond water or water that has stabilised in an aquarium. Cover one end with black sugar paper and place a pond snail in the centre of the container. Shine a bright light on to the water. Check after 15 minutes to find out if the snail is in the bright or dimly-lit end of the box.

Repeat the experiment a number of times, using a fresh snail of the same species each time. Do snails prefer bright or dim light?

Up for air

Water boatmen come to the surface of the pond for air. Watch a water boatman in a jam jar of pond water and time it for 30 minutes.

How often does it come to the surface for air? The frequency depends upon the temperature of the water and on the activity of the boatman.

Exploring food webs

The interdependence of living things shows up well in any discussion on food webs found in a pond.

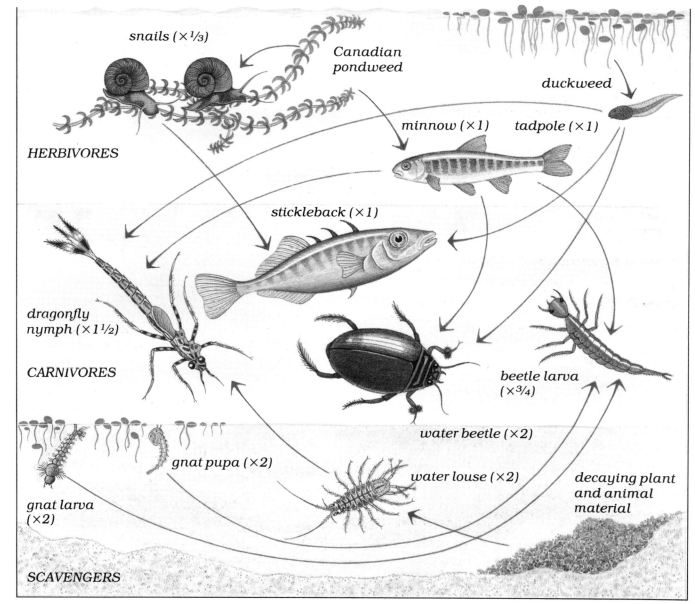

snails (×⅓)

Canadian pondweed

duckweed

minnow (×1)   tadpole (×1)

HERBIVORES

stickleback (×1)

dragonfly nymph (×1½)

CARNIVORES

beetle larva (×¾)

water beetle (×2)

gnat pupa (×2)

gnat larva (×2)

water louse (×2)

decaying plant and animal material

SCAVENGERS

Tracks and trails of animals in gardens, parks, woods, on the seashore and in streets are often found. Marks stand out particularly well in mud, sand or snow.

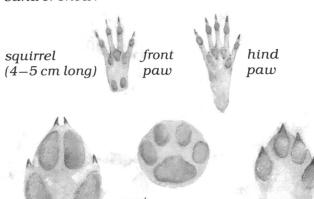

squirrel
(4—5 cm long)

front paw

hind paw

fox
(4—5 cm across)

cat
(retracted claws
3—4 cm across)

rabbit
(6—9 cm long)

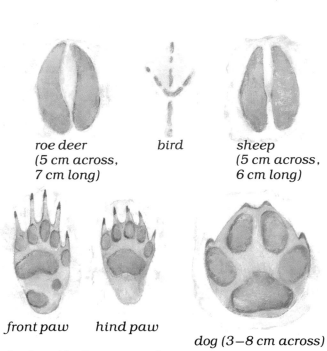

roe deer
(5 cm across,
7 cm long)

bird

sheep
(5 cm across,
6 cm long)

front paw

hind paw

badger (4—6 cm across)

dog (3—8 cm across)

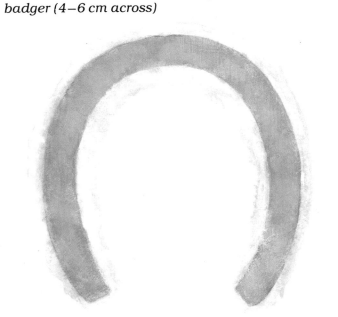

horse (unshod over 11.5 cm across)

horse (shod)

Make some records

Draw the track and make measurements.

Trace the shape of the track on to clear plastic, using a black felt tip pen.

Make some plaster casts too (see page 7).

Food signs

Bark stripped from trees gives evidence of rabbits, deer or bank voles. The height at which the bark is stripped, as well as the actual teethmarks, show which animals have been busy.

Here are some other signs.

rabbit droppings

hazelnuts eaten by a woodmouse

acorn eaten by a rabbit

fir cone with the scales stripped off by a squirrel

straight cuts in the leaf made by a snail's radula

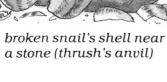

broken snail's shell near a stone (thrush's anvil)

barn owl pellet

leaf miners make pale-coloured tunnels as they feed

Different types of sign

feathers

sheep's wool on fences

egg shell thrown from a nest

cast snake's skin

neat round pieces cut by a leaf-cutting bee to make its nest

orb-web of a spider

hammock web of a spider

bird's nest

What makes up soil?

Soil is made of different sized particles and contains decaying plant and other organic matter called humus.

Collect a number of soils from a variety of places: the edge of a lawn, a garden bed, underneath a tree. Put a sample of each soil in its own jam jar to a depth of 3 cm. Use similar jam jars.
Add a 6 cm depth of water, stir well and leave to settle. The heavier particles will settle first. How do your soils compare? Woodland soil, for example, may have a high leaf litter content, while a heathland soil will be lacking humus.

soil from a flower bed   *soil from a lawn*

soil from a vegetable plot

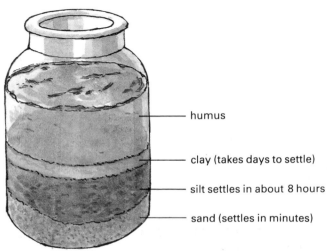

humus

clay (takes days to settle)

silt settles in about 8 hours

sand (settles in minutes)

Measuring soil water

Take each of the soils collected from different places and weigh out 500 g of each.

Place each in a separate bowl and allow it to dry in a warm place. Reweigh.

Do some soils hold more water than others?

A soil window

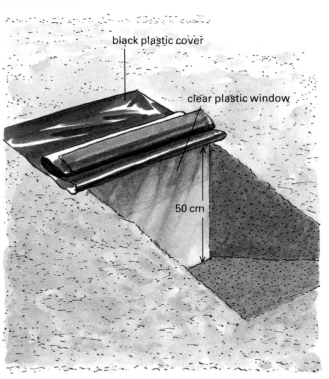

black plastic cover

clear plastic window

50 cm

Keep the window in the dark, except when making observations. In time, plant roots should show clearly against the window and you may see worm burrows and traces of other animals.

You should also be able to see the soil layers which show up as different colours, the humus being much darker than the soil beneath.

Feeling soils

Soils can be smooth, sharp, silky, sticky, damp or gritty. Use this key to separate them by touch.

A

Damp soil rolled between two hands forms a cylinder — B

Damp soil rolled between two hands does not form a cylinder — sand

B

Cylinder of soil can be twisted into a ring — clay

Cylinder of soil cannot be twisted into a ring — C

C

Soil feels smooth and silky — clay loam

Soil feels gritty — sandy loam

Looking at soil animals

Use a Tullgren funnel to extract small animals from the soil.

table lamp with
25 watt bulb
to slowly dry
the soil

coarse kitchen sieve
clamped to the table
(2 mm holes)

brown paper funnel
taped to the sieve

jam jar lined with
damp blotting paper

Rich soil from a garden bed is best for this. Pile the soil sample in the centre of the sieve, leaving a gap around the edge so that air can circulate and dry the soil out. Switch on the lamp. As the soil dries out, the animals slowly migrate downward and fall into the funnel.

Examine the jar two or three times a day. A binocular microscope is useful for looking at the smaller animals. Compare animals from different soils and animals from different depths. Return the animals to the soil afterwards.

Measure water holding

Spread some sand, clay and loam soils on a newspaper to dry. Break up any lumps. Test the water-retaining capacity of each, using this home-made apparatus.

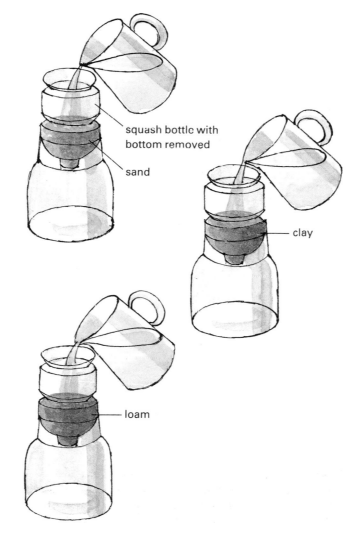

squash bottle with
bottom removed

sand

clay

loam

Of course, you should keep the amount of soil and water constant in each case to ensure that a fair test is made.

Test fertilizers

Use a chequerboard garden to test the effect of fertilizers. Make each plot a quarter metre square and compare potatoes grown with farmyard manure against those grown with Growmore.

The nutrient elements in soil, especially nitrogen, phosphorus and potassium become depleted. Fertilizers are designed to replace these elements. They are usually intended to be complementary to organic manuring, for soil fertility is dependent on decomposing organic material which forms humus.

So try both manure and Growmore.

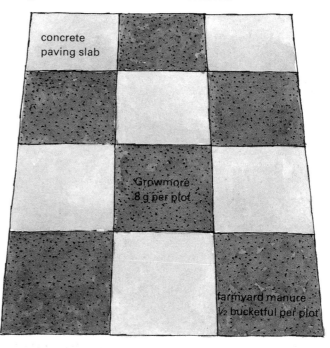

concrete
paving slab

Growmore
8 g per plot

farmyard manure
½ bucketful per plot

Try three separate plots of radishes. Use sulphate of ammonia (high in nitrogen) on one plot, superphosphate on the second, and sulphate of potash (high in potassium) on the third. Nitrogen promotes leaf growth and phosphorus helps good root development.

The terrain of the moon can be seen quite clearly through a telescope or binoculars. The main features are the flat areas (or seas), the mountains, the craters, and the radial lines (or rays) surrounding the craters. The moon always presents the same surface to the earth.

Charting the position of the moon throughout the month is best done by taking observations facing south, with east to your left and west to your right. You will not be able to see the moon until two or three days after new moon.

Stand in the same spot each time to record your observations. Draw what you observe against an outline picture of the landscape, recording the time of each observation. Use dotted lines for observations made in daylight and solid lines for observations made during darkness.

Show the age of the moon in days from the first appearance of the new moon. If the moon is seen in daylight during the afternoon then it is waxing. If it is seen in daylight during the early morning then it is waning.

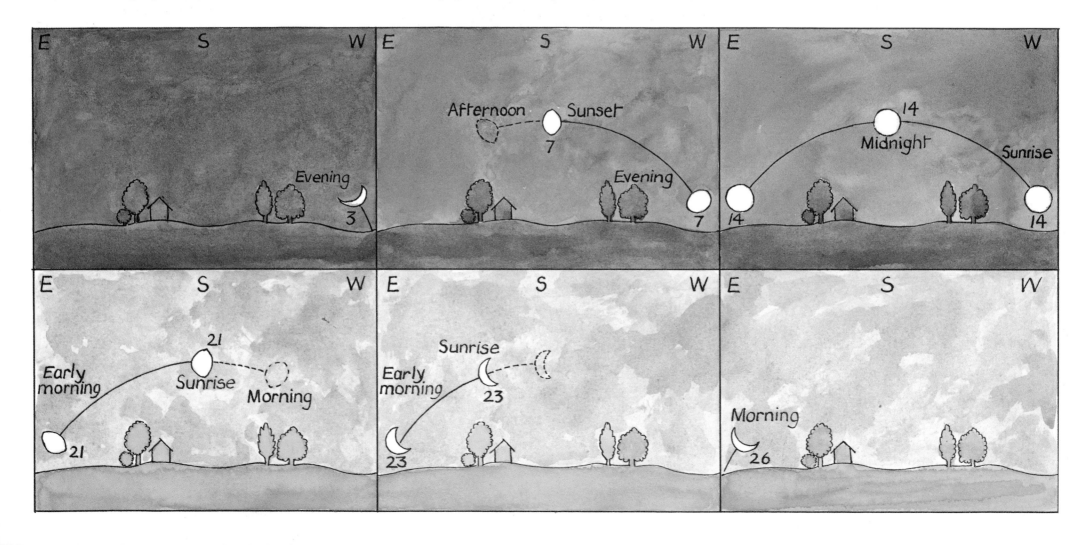

Looking at constellations

Star patterns, or constellations, are fairly easy to identify.

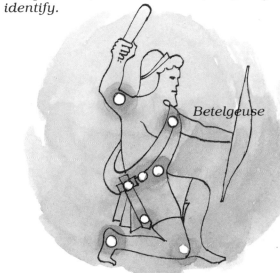

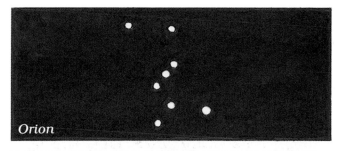

Orion

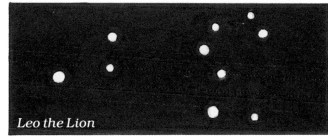

Leo the Lion

The winter sky is dominated by Orion, the hunter, with the reddish-orange supergiant Betelgeuse in his left shoulder. The three stars in Orion's belt point downwards to Sirius, the Dog Star. This seems very bright because it is one of the stars nearest to us.

Try pricking out some constellations on pieces of black sugar paper. Mount them on a window pane with Blue-tak.

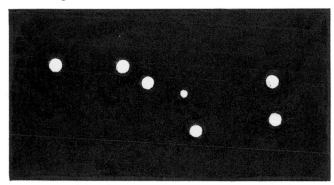

The Plough

The pattern of the stars in the night sky alters as the night passes.

Turn your star patterns against the light. Can you identify them still?

Make a star clock

The revolution of the earth every 24 hours means that the stars change their position in the night sky. You can use these changes to tell the time.

Make a clock using two circular pieces of card, 20 cm and 15 cm in diameter. Mark the outer edge of the larger card with the 24-hour clock, marking numbers every 15 degrees. Draw a circle of diameter 10 cm on the inner piece of card. The hands of the clock could be the two constellations called the Plough and Cassiopeia. Draw these in relation to each other and to the Pole Star, which would be at the centre of the clock. Fix the two pieces of card together with a paper fastener.

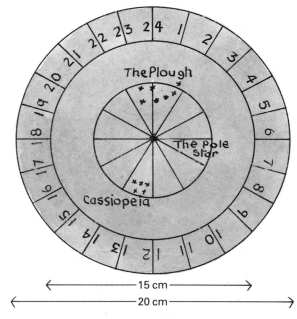

To use the clock, match the constellations drawn on the card with the constellations in the sky. Place the clock on a window-sill, maintaining these positions. An hour later, match your clock against the constellations in the sky by rotating the clock by 15 degrees.

Identification books

Keble-Martin W. (1965), *The Concise British Flora in Colour*, Michael Joseph

McClintock D. and Fitter R.S.R. (1956), *Collins Pocket Guide to Wild Flowers*, Collins

Nicholson B.E., Wallis M., Anderson E., Balfour A., Fish M., and Finnis B. (1963), *The Oxford Book of Garden Flowers*, Oxford University Press

Vedel H. and Lange J. (1960), *Trees and Bushes, in Wood and Hedgerow*, Metheun

Brightman F.M. and Nicholson B.E. (1966), *The Oxford Book of Flowerless Plants*, Oxford University Press

Hyde M. (1976), *Hedgerow Plants*, Shire Publications

Chinery M. (1973), *A Field Guide to the Insects of Britain and Northern Europe*, Collins

Barrett J. and Yonge C.M. (1976), *Collins Pocket Guide to the Seashore*, Collins

Peterson R., Mountfort G. and Hollom P.A.D. (1983), *A Field Guide to the Birds of Britain and Europe*, Collins

Bang P. and Dahlstrom P. (1974), *Animal Tracks and Signs*, Collins

Stars at a Glance: A Simple Guide to the Heavens, 2nd edn, 1959, Philip

Identification books specifically for children

The Clue Books
Authors: G.R. Allen and J.B. Denslow
Publishers: Oxford University Press

Bones	*Freshwater Animals*
Birds	*Seashore Animals*
Flowers	*Flowerless Plants*
Insects	*Tracks and Signs*
Trees	

Learning Through Science Pupils' Packs
Publishers: Macdonald

Which and What

Publications for teachers

School Natural Science Society Pamphlets
Available from:

The Association for Science Education
College Lane
Hatfield
Herts AL10 9AA

Centre for Life Studies Booklets
Available from:

The Warden
Centre for Life Studies
Zoological Gardens
Regents Park
London NW1 4RY

Learning Through Science Pupils' Packs
Publishers: Macdonald

All Around
Out of Doors
On the Move
Sky and Space

Science 5/13
Publishers: Macdonald

Minibeasts
Trees

Suppliers of apparatus and materials

E.J. Arnold & Son Ltd
Dewsbury Road
Leeds LS11 5TD
Telephone: 0532 772112

Griffin & George Ltd
Bishops Meadow Road
Loughborough
Leicestershire LE11 0RG
Telephone: 0509 233344

Philip Harris Ltd
Lynn Lane
Shenstone
Staffordshire WS14 0EE
Telephone: 0543 480077

Osmiroid International Ltd
Fareham Road
Gosport
Hampshire PO13 0A1
Telephone: 0329 232345

Useful societies

The Young Ornithologists' Club
Royal Society for the Protection of Birds
The Lodge
Sandy
Bedfordshire SG21 2DL

WATCH
Royal Society for Nature Conservation
The Green
Nettleham
Lincoln